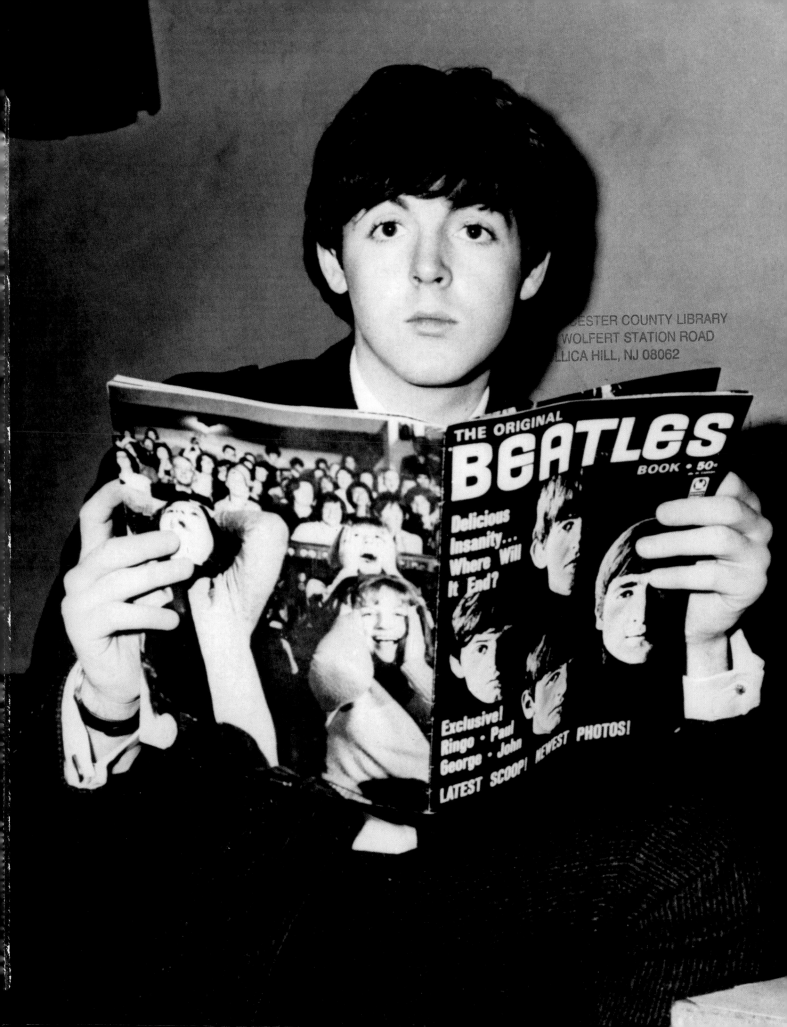

THE ORIGINAL
BEATLES
BOOK • 50¢

Delicious
Insanity...
Where Will
It End?

Exclusive!
Ringo • Paul
George • John

LATEST SCOOP! NEWEST PHOTOS!

PAUL

by Tony Scherman
and the
Editors of LIFE

Special Photographic
Portfolio by
Harry Benson

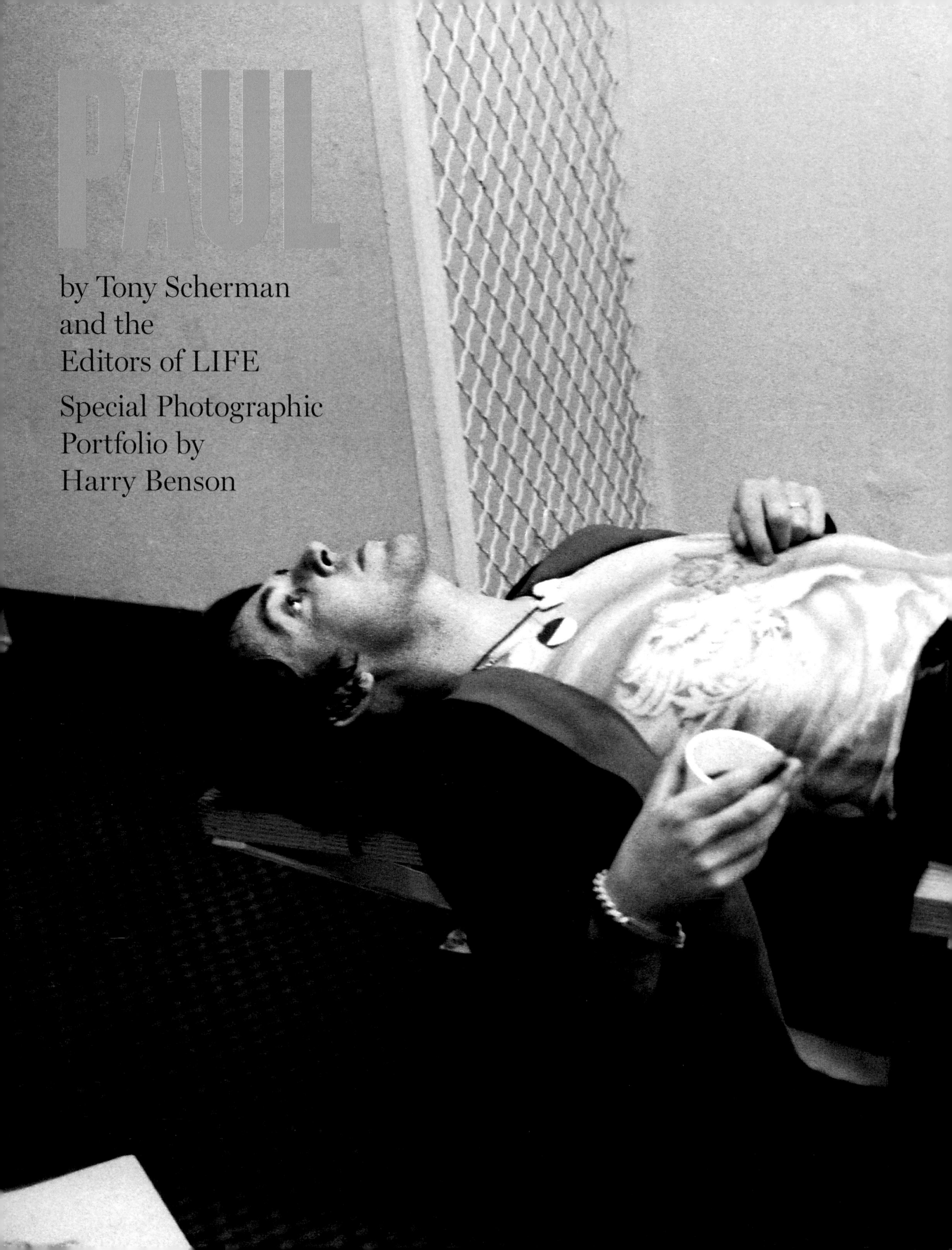

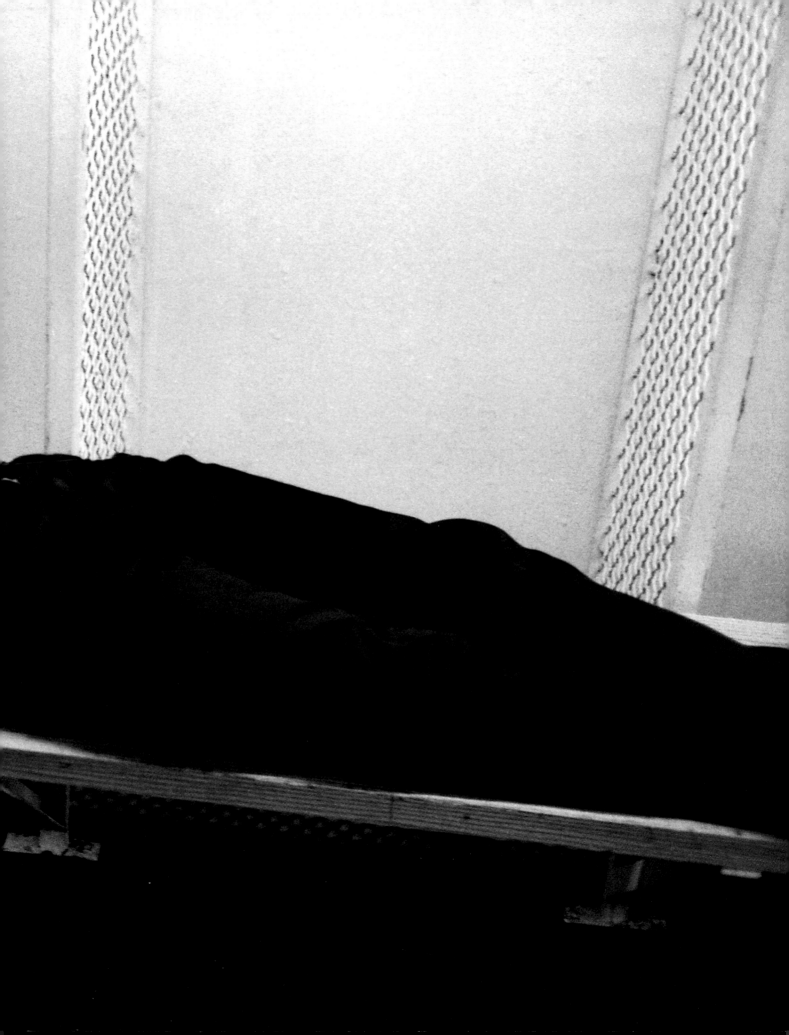

PAUL

LIFE BOOKS

Managing Editor
Robert Sullivan

Director of Photography
Barbara Baker Burrows

Creative Direction
Li'l Robin Design, Inc.

Deputy Picture Editor
Christina Lieberman

Writer-Reporters
Amy Lennard Goehner (Chief),
Marilyn Fu, Christine M. Gordon,
Daniel S. Levy

Copy Chief
Barbara Gogan

Copy Editors
Don Armstrong, Parlan McGaw

Associate Picture Editor
Sarah Cates

Photo Assistant
Jehan Jillani

Consulting Picture Editors
Mimi Murphy (Rome),
Tala Skari (Paris)

Editorial Director
Stephen Koepp

TIME INC. PREMEDIA

Richard K. Prue (Director), Brian
Fellows (Manager), Richard
Shaffer (Production), Keith
Aurelio, Jen Brown, Charlotte
Coco, Liz Grover, Kevin Hart, Mert
Kerimoglu, Rosalie Khan, Patricia
Koh, Marco Lau, Brian Mai, Po
Fung Ng, Rudi Papiri, Robert
Pizaro, Barry Pribula, Clara
Renauro, Vaune Trachtman

TIME HOME ENTERTAINMENT

President
Jim Childs

**Vice President, Brand & Digital
Strategy** Steven Sandonato

Executive Director, Marketing Services
Carol Pittard

**Executive Director, Retail & Special
Sales** Tom Mifsud

Executive Publishing Director
Joy Butts

**Director, Bookazine Development
& Marketing** Laura Adam

Finance Director
Glenn Buonocore

Publishing Director
Megan Pearlman

Associate General Counsel
Helen Wan

Assistant Director, Special Sales
Ilene Schreider

Senior Book Production Manager
Susan Chodakiewicz

Brand Manager
Roshni Patel

Associate Prepress Manager
Alex Voznesenskiy

Associate Project Manager
Stephanie Braga

Copy Chief
Rina Bander

Design Manager
Anne-Michelle Gallero

Special thanks: Katherine Barnet,
Brad Beatson, Jeremy Biloon,
Dana Campolattaro, Rose
Cirrincione, Natalie Ebel, Assu
Etsubneh, Mariana Evans,
Christine Font, Susan Hettlema
Hillary Hirsch, David Kahn, Amy
Mangus, Kimberly Marshall, Nir
Mistry, Dave Rozzelle, Ricardo
Santiago, Gina Scauzillo, Adrian
Tierno, Vanessa Wu

Page 1: Reading a fanzine in 1965
that features ominous cover cop
PHOTOGRAPH FROM MICHAEL OCH
ARCHIVES/GETTY.

Pages 2–3: Recovering in Phoenix
during a Wings tour in 1976.
PHOTOGRAPH BY © HARRY BENSON

These pages: Sitting on a bench in
Hyde Park, London, April 1966.
PHOTOGRAPH BY JEAN-MARIE
PÉRIER/PHOTO12/POLARIS.

Harry Benson was omnipresent with the Beatles even before the invasion of America 50 years ago, having made, for instance, the famous pillow fight sequence at the George V hotel in Paris in 1964 (please see page 104). Much later, he was still with Paul, fashioning, for instance, the lying-down shot on our title pages (pages two and three), taken during a Wings tour in 1976. Below: Harry as a Beatle in 1964, with the unseen John releasing the shutter on Harry's camera. On the opposite page, he is with Paul in 1975 (top) and in 1992 (bottom).

a period spent working for LIFE in various trouble spots around the world. He was met at the airport by his 13-year-old daughter, Cara, who gushed, "Dad, Dad, you've got to do a story on those fab Beatles!" Spencer, who died in 2009, remembered in a 2005 interview with LIFE: "As I'd never heard of them, my reaction was pretty much, 'Oh God, what's she on about now?'" He soon found out and was able to chronicle the excitement as the first wave of Beatlemania swept across England and Europe. He told LIFE's editors in New York what he had—and that this was something very new. They said, in effect: "Yeah, sure." When Pan Am Flight 101 landed at the newly renamed John F. Kennedy International Airport in New York 50 years ago, LIFE sent staff photographer Bill Eppridge out to Queens to record the scene, but only a few of his shots ran.

Very quickly, LIFE was playing catch-up. After the New York City tsunami that included the appearance on *The Ed Sullivan Show*,

in the U.S. to a crazed crowd of 7,000. Then the Beatles were taken to Florida to chill, and LIFE's John Loengard took his famous photograph of them in a swimming pool on a chilly day in Miami Beach (please see page 53). Later that year, when the Beatles returned for their second American visit, LIFE deemed them cover-worthy, and John Dominis made the happy portrait that appears in this introduction and first appeared on the cover of our August 28, 1964, edition.

There's an oft-told anecdote in our halls that when Eppridge was on the tarmac on the day of the Beatles' arrival, he and other photographers were debating the best position for just the right shot. Then the plane landed, the stairs came out, the Beatles descended and a photographer with a head of wavy hair appeared in the doorway and ordered the lads to turn and wave. Eppridge or someone else pointed at him and said, "Right there! That's the place to be." They were right, and Harry Benson's photograph is

the best known from that day (please see page 106). The young Scotsman working for a Fleet Street paper in London was unknown to LIFE at the time, but he became a valued contributor and dear friend in subsequent years. He is also the rare chronicler who was with Paul early and late, and when assembling this book a very first thought was: "a Harry portfolio." And so our volume is distinguished by his special pictures, embellished by his reminiscences.

Finally, who to write the narrative? Again we went to our LIFE team. Tony Scherman's father, David, was one of the storied LIFE photographers of the World War II era, and Tony wrote many fine features and profiles for the monthly LIFE in the 1990s. He is not only the author of acclaimed books on Andy Warhol and R&B drummer Earl Palmer but is a talented drummer himself. His take on Paul can be considered an admiring, critical look at the man. Some of Tony's musical assessments, which

enliven the text from time to time, are open to debate. But then: LIFE's coverage of the Beatles has been thus from the start.

We're still catching up.

PAUL

His Long and Winding Road
By Tony Scherman

In 1964.

t is April 17, 2009 (although the scene has been replicated even more recently), and Paul McCartney is onstage, closing Day One of the 10th annual Coachella Festival, three days of rock 'n' roll in the Southern California desert. This is McCartney's first visit to Coachella, which is perhaps the most successful and sane of the scores of post–Woodstock/Altamont/Watkins Glen open-air rock-outs staged for "the kids." Handing off his bass and strapping on a Gibson Les Paul guitar, McCartney whangs on the strings until he's kicked the band into overdrive, his guitar pyrotechnics a reminder that it was he, not George, who played the solos 40-plus years ago on "Taxman," "Good Morning, Good Morning," "Back in the USSR," "Helter Skelter" and half a dozen others. The guitar isn't even Paul's main instrument, but he likes to play it. He likes to play anything.

Two days later, as the trucks are still being packed and the debris cleared, *New York Times* critic Ben Ratliff, as part of his festival roundup, picks his five highlights out of this year's 176 acts, most of whom are young enough to be McCartney's grandkids, and writes of "Paul McCartney's electric guitar solos, smoking much of the competition." Sir Paul is about to turn 67 (never mind "when I'm 64").

Today he's 71. His newest album, *New*, is new indeed—fresh, Beatlesque rock. His previous collection was a set of cover versions of mostly American standards. He has become a man of many parts—and admits to all of them.

The last Beatle out there (though every now and then, Ringo hits the road with the most recent incarnation of the All Starr Band for an evening of nostalgia and laughs), McCartney has been making music for more than half a century, or since he was 14. He first picked up the guitar (it would take him five years to make an unplanned switch to the bass) to console himself over the death of his adored mother, whose name, Mary, echoes in one of Paul's signature songs, "Let It Be." John Lennon's ballad "Julia" was also written for a lost mother. John lost Julia Lennon twice. After more or

Mike and Paul McCartney, circa 1947, on a Welsh hillside. Mike, who would have a career as a rock photographer, fronted a music-poetry-comedy act for more than a decade in the 1960s and '70s that had a No. 1 hit in the U.K. His stage name was Mike McGear—*gear* (derived from the French *de rigueur*, according to John Lennon) being a synonym in Liverpool for "cool" or "fab"—as he didn't want to trade on the famous surname.

less abandoning her son when he was five, she was fatally struck by a car. John was 17. "That was our biggest bond," said Paul—"our mums had died when we were teenagers."

Music, Paul discovered in the wake of his loss, helped him to release emotions that would otherwise have remained bottled up. After a tentative start, he surrendered completely to music-making, to the point of bringing his guitar into the loo with him and sitting and playing for hours. (Just by the way, since rock 'n' roll tradition hovers everywhere here, Paul wasn't the only teenage strummer to adopt this practice—on the road at 15, Robbie Robertson, later the Band's fine guitarist, often vanished into motel johns to hone his chops in private.) Paul's younger brother, Mike, recalled of Paul's years of self-tutelage: "He was lost in another world. It was useless talking to him. I had better conversations with brick walls."

So music was everything for Paul since he was a conflicted, ambitious boy. It seems it still is; he remains so driven. One day he's at Tony Bennett's high school in Queens, New York, performing for the students there, the next he's in Times Square delivering a free concert, online the next chatting with fans about the new recording, probably planning the follow-up that night. He says he can't imagine not doing it, and that statement is easily taken at face value. It's remarkable that Paul can still hit the high notes of 1970's "Maybe I'm Amazed" or write the first-rate songs on the new album *New*. Considering the facts—that Elvis ended so sadly, that John ended more sadly still, that Dylan's voice has grown less melodious than a frog's, that the Stones have been coasting since the '80s—no one has gone through the fire that McCartney has and is so successfully carrying on. There has never been anyone like Paul McCartney.

The first act is the one to focus on most intently.

Paul and Mike's mother, Mary, would die of an embolism after an operation for breast cancer in 1956 at age 47. Paul said later, "My mother's death broke my dad up. That was the worst thing for me, hearing my dad cry." Motherless, he said, he "grew up quick." Mary was the inspiration for the song "Let It Be."

Christened James Paul McCartney, the first of James and Mary McCartney's two children, he was born on June 18, 1942. Jim McCartney was a better-than-average piano player (despite being deaf in one ear), an occasional songwriter and the leader of a World War I–era dance band, the Masked Melody Makers, who also accompanied silent movies at the local cinema. They quickly discarded their masks and, necessarily, their name, when they realized that their sweat was making the masks bleed black dye all over their faces. The McCartney family's musicales had more or less stopped by the time Paul was born, but Jim kept on playing piano, and later tried to convince young Paul to take the lessons he'd never had. Paul refused; he wanted to teach himself, and by ear (and as fine a multi-instrumentalist as he became, he has never learned how to

read music). Yet Paul isn't exactly self-taught. He may not have taken his father's advice, but he spent many hours watching over his father's shoulder—studying Jim's hands and the keys, and how these two elements produced a third element: organized sound. Music. Jim McCartney's music is where his son's begins.

Paul McCartney's hometown, and that of all the Beatles, is Liverpool, a once-bustling English seaport two hundred miles north-west of London. Liverpool is the largest of five municipalities lying within the county of Merseyside, historically a loosely defined geographic area. In the days of Paul's childhood, Liverpool, with 750,000 residents, was Britain's fourth most populous city, its busiest deep-water port, and the home of one of the largest grain terminals and cotton markets in Europe. In the first third of the 20th century and earlier, members of Liverpool's large

John's band is evolving. The front man is singing, opposite, top, circa 1958 (Paul, new to the group, is at the other microphone). Bottom: After George's brother Harry has married in 1958, the wedding band, the Quarry Men, poses during a break at the reception at the Childwall Abbey Hotel in Liverpool. Above: Paul and John play to the (close-at-hand) crowd in the Rainbow Room of a Liverpool nightspot called the Casbah Coffee Club in 1959. The fan in the floral dress who has eyes for "the cute one" is Cynthia Powell, who will marry John in 1962.

working class, most of them employed on the docks, were enormously proud of their city and its vintage—it was founded in 1207—and ready to stoutly defend its honor.

World War II took the better part of Liverpool's energy and prosperity with it. Business began to slacken, at first barely perceptibly, then with alarming speed. Thousands of residents drifted off in search of employment. The docking industry, employing 60,000 in its heyday and so vital to the city's economic health, moved to more promising locales. As Liverpool's prosperity faded, so did its residents' famous cheeky optimism.

Some of that spirit reemerged in the mid-'50s from an unexpected source. Postwar Britain's first music to excite its teenagers was a folk-, blues- and jazz-based style known as skiffle (originally a synonym for rent party), whose appeal to aspiring players was the ease with which it could be learned and its affordability—it was played on homemade instruments: washboard, jugs, tea-chest bass, cigar-box fiddle, saw and kazoo, as well as the occasional mail-order guitar.

Skiffle's popularity was short-lived. In 1956, the music's superstar, Scotsman Lonnie Donegan, had a big hit with a dreadful cover of Leadbelly's "Rock Island Line." Two years later, skiffle slunk away—too ratty, too dog-eared, too ramshackle. Something else was just over the horizon—a giant rogue wave crossing the Atlantic to rise to a tremendous height and slowly break over England.

In Liverpool in 1957, three underachieving teenagers happened to meet, in different months and different parts of town. These were chance meetings, but in hindsight it is as if these three had sought each other out. On the bus to Inny (the Liverpool Institute), his grammar school, 14-year-old Paul McCartney met a pint-size, snaggletoothed 13-year-old with a pompadour, a cocky sprat from working-class Speke. George Harrison's father was a bus driver and a stalwart union man. It speaks

In Hamburg, Germany, circa 1960, Stuart Sutcliffe is in the background and Paul is to the fore. With Stuart's exit from the band (which would be followed by his tragically early death from a brain hemorrhage), Paul would switch from six-string guitar to bass.

Certainly when Stu Sutcliffe (in shades), Paul, George and Pete Best share space at a monument in the Netherlands with three associates (the group's manager, Allan Williams; his wife, Beryl; Williams's business partner, calypso singer Lord Woodbine), in a photo snapped by John Lennon, they take the inscribed motto as humorous, ironic. They are living a gritty-in-the-extreme existence, sharing a heritage of unfinished education and being paid peanuts. That their names might live forevermore? There is nothing to indicate such. Life can be funny.

to Paul's pleasant and basically nonjudgmental character that he didn't condescend to little George. On the contrary, the two became mates, taking in a Lonnie Donegan concert together. Through a happy accident, George played guitar. Less of a natural talent than Paul, George had to work a good deal harder—his mother recalled many days of bloody fingertips and howls of frustrated rage.

Unlike Paul and George, with their blue-collar upbringings, John Winston Lennon (the middle name was for the World War II hero and prime minister; too warlike and aristocratic for the adult Lennon's taste, he later changed it to Ono) was raised on Liverpool's cozy, bourgeois Menlove Avenue, although he later grew fond of presenting himself as working class—witness his 1970 dirge/anthem "Working Class Hero."

John was born in 1940, the only child of two feckless parents, Freddie and Julia Lennon, who passed John off at five to Julia's efficient and caring older sister, John's aunt Mimi (under the circumstances, a lifesaving act). As a teenager, John affected the look and air of a teddy boy, postwar England's rebels without a cause: swept-back hair, skintight jeans and hard-boiled, caustic manner calculated to always appear on the verge of violence. The teds' call to arms was the 1955 American movie *Blackboard Jungle*. During a 1956 showing in south London, they rioted, ripping theater seats out of the floor and dancing in the aisles. After this widely publicized display of antisocial

Some historians might disagree, but there's not a lot in it, this transformation from late-stages Quarry Men (who had already forsaken skiffle for rock 'n' roll) to Silver Beetles to Beatles playing their first shows at Liverpool's Cavern—in other words, from the photo above to the one at right.

behavior, riots occurred all over England whenever *Blackboard Jungle* was shown. (In 2007, the *Journal of Criminal Justice and Popular Culture* published an article analyzing the movie's connection to juvenile delinquency.)

In 1956, John was a rank beginner on guitar, using just four strings on his mail-order special, when he put together a sextet he named the Quarry Men, after Quarry Bank, the high school that he and his bandmates attended. The Quarry Men played skiffle, with a few exploratory stabs at rock. John's contrary sense of humor was perhaps the combo's dominant feature. In the Quarry Men's repertoire was one of early rock 'n' roll's big hits, the Del-Vikings' "Come Go with Me." Not really on top of the lyrics, John made up his own:

Come go with me
To the penitentiary . . .

According to Paul, he and John met cute, sort of. "At Woolton village fete I met him," begins Paul's introduction to *In His Own Write*, John's slim, pun-filled 1964 best-seller. "I was a fat schoolboy," continues Paul, "and as he leaned an arm on my shoulder, I realized that he was drunk."

Paul seems to have blurred the sequence of events. What likely happened is that after the Woolton fete, the Quarry Men had a gig in the Village Hall, just across the street. A kid nobody knew, quite the "toff" in a white sports jacket and tie, asked to sit in. Borrowing a guitar, he launched into, first, Eddie Cochran's tongue-twisting, amateur-killing "Twenty Flight Rock." Moving to the piano, the kid raced through Little Richard's "Long Tall Sally," hitting all of Richard's signature falsetto notes just like Richard. The Quarry Men were speechless.

"It was uncanny," said Quarry Man Eric Griffiths. "He could play and sing in a way that none of us could, including John. He had such confidence; he gave a *performance*. We couldn't get enough of it."

The multi-instrumentalist ball of fire was Paul, of course. Shortly afterward, he was walking down the street when a Quarry Man named Pete Shotton, a good friend of Lennon's and an obvious emissary, approached Paul and asked if he wanted to join the band. Tired of playing in his room, Paul leapt at the offer.

In Paul's first days with the Quarry Men, John kept his distance, eyeing the newcomer warily—Paul was so clearly the better musician, and despite having invited Paul into the band, John was worried about his place in the pecking order. Yet if competitiveness developed, it bore fruit. "It was a good competitiveness," said Bill Harry, a friend of John's who founded the rock journal *Mersey Beat*. "'I'm going to beat you, but I'm not going to beat you as an enemy. We're in the competition together. I'll win one day, and you'll win the other.'" A strong affinity developed between the two gifted bandmates, its components a love of rock 'n' roll, a determination to avoid their fellow Liverpudlians' lackluster existences and, as noted earlier, the nagging hurt they shared as the sons of mothers who died too young. Far from static, the pair's relationship could be steeped in loathing one day, fondness the next. The only constant was its intensity. Their mutual emotions forged the strongest bond in each other's lives until the arrival of Yoko and Linda.

McCartney biographer Howard Sounes depicted a stunned Paul reading what Lennon, who for years he'd considered his best friend, had to say about him in Lennon's epochal 1971 interview with Jann Wenner of *Rolling Stone*: "McCartney read with horrified fascination how he'd taken over the leadership of the Beatles after Brian Epstein died, only to lead the band 'round in circles' while John, George and Ringo had been made to feel like his sidemen." In the years immediately following the group's 1970 breakup, the fondness evaporated. You can hear the depth of John's hostility in his 1971 diatribe, "How Do You Sleep?" The song boils over with something like loathing—"The only thing you done was yesterday"—with a viciousness that, even given the difficult circumstances, feels somehow exaggerated. Whence so much rancor? However, for the better part of the foursome's decade together, Paul's belief in his and John's rapport had been justified. And despite the bitter conflicts and phases of mutual dislike that came after the breakup, their love for each other never vanished completely.

Jim McCartney, seen here in 1960 with his boys, Paul and Mike, was, like his late wife, Mary, and many other Liverpudlians, of Irish heritage. He worked most of his life in the cotton trade. Not long after this photograph is taken, in 1964, he marries a widow named Angela Williams and adopts her daughter, Ruth, so Paul and Mike have a stepsister. Once the Beatles make it big, Jim bids the council-house life goodbye as Paul buys him a proper estate in Cheshire that they call Rembrandt. Jim McCartney, his sons' first great musical influence, dies in 1976.

John's most evident trait was his caustic wit, verging at times on sadistic. "If he could humiliate you," said a childhood friend, "he would." Paul, on the other hand, was polite and considerate. In fact, the two friends were the opposite of what they seemed. John's jeering exterior masked an easily wounded inner self. And a casual acquaintance with well-mannered Paul would not lead you to guess that this was a tough, stubborn character who wouldn't hesitate to elbow you into the ditch if you were in the way. Of the pair, Paul clearly had the surer, less conflicted relationship with success.

They met daily ("John, your little friend's here!" Aunt Mimi would announce). Paul gave John guitar lessons; they taught each other songs, worked out primitive versions of the envied Beatles harmonies and took apart the music of the American rockers they loved: Little Richard, Chuck Berry, Eddie Cochran, Gene Vincent and, of course, Elvis.

In 1958, John's Quarry Bank class graduated and his bandmates peeled off, looking for jobs, their flirtation with the musician's life over. As for John, he was in this for the duration. Paul wasn't sure. Still saddled with a need for conventional success and for pleasing his father (these amounted to the same thing), Paul considered enrolling in teacher-training college. For the time being, he was half of the Quarry Men; he and John were all that remained of the former sextet. They played rock 'n' roll now, skiffle having become an object of disdain.

At Paul's encouragement, his friend George Harrison started showing up at Quarry Men gigs with his guitar, venturing up to the side of the stage (when there was a stage) as the two older kids played. Now and then he tossed off a flashy little Chet Atkins or Scotty Moore lick. Finally deigning to acknowledge George's presence, John fixed him with a condescending stare, then ignored him again. But George so clearly ached to join that John, relinquishing his usual approach with the vulnerable—ridicule and embarrass—told the youngster that, all right, he could have a tryout. Paul, who'd been faking obliviousness, flashed George a smile. And as Paul knew he would,

14-year-old George fit right in. The one thing dampening George's excitement was the others' superior attitude. They were the leaders; he would never be more than "the guitar player." It was a gripe of George's that lasted as long as the Beatles did.

By 1958, three quarters of the Beatles were on board. All of that time together playing parties, dances and fly-by-night clubs explains the threesome's (Ringo was a relative latecomer) mutual near-clairvoyance, each one's ability to intuit what the others were going to play almost before they essayed it.

This brand-new rock 'n' roll trio—no bassist, no drummer—plied Merseyside, taking whatever gigs came its way. On September 18, 1959, a front-page story in the suburban *West Derby Reporter*, covering the opening of the Casbah Coffee Club, a gathering place for teenagers, mentioned "a guitar group which entertains the club members on Saturday nights . . . The group, who call themselves 'The Quarry Men' . . . are: John Lennon, Menlove Avenue, Woolton; Paul McCartney, Forthlin Road, Allerton; and George Harrison, Upton Green, Speke."

In mid-1959, Stuart Sutcliffe, a gifted painter and a friend of John's from the Liverpool College of Art (from which John narrowly missed flunking out after his second year) began coming to band rehearsals and gigs.

At Lennon's urging, Sutcliffe, who had no musical talent whatsoever, put all of his earnings from a recent sale into a high-end Hofner electric bass. Under John's supervision, Stu began to teach himself, and made no progress, playing everything out of tune and at the wrong tempo. Perhaps the only explanation for so total a failure to advance on a melodic/harmonic instrument despite much time put in is tone-deafness. But Stu *looked* great, said John, in response to Paul's disgusted complaints. John was still the nominal leader, and Stu stayed.

Then there was the matter of a new name. John and Paul were sick of "the Quarry Men," with its connection to skiffle. Better that it sounds . . . contemporary. Wait—John has it! Johnny & the Moondogs—as in Dion and the Belmonts, Vito and the Salutations, Johnny Maestro and the Crests, all those New York vocal groups with their magical names,

Opposite are two scenes from Hamburg before the rush to fame in England: At the Top Ten Club (top) and the larger Star-Club. Usually, when it was time to add an instrument, like piano, Paul got the nod. Everyone in the band realized he was the best, most gifted musician; even John never quarreled with that assessment. Interestingly, though, Paul has never become the master of keyboards that he is of all manner of guitar.

looks and sound. The three others shrugged, said nothing. By default, then, Johnny & the Moondogs it was.

Not for long, as was the case with all of the group's name choices. At the start of 1960, they were searching once more. A friend of Lennon's named Bill Harry came across John and Stuart Sutcliffe in a pub. "We're auditioning names," said Lennon. "C'mon, you can help." They wanted something that made one think of Buddy Holly and the Crickets, Lennon told Harry. They went through a plethora of insect names, finally arriving at "beetles," which, for the time being, was as far as they got. For the next few months, they called themselves Beetles, Silver Beetles, Silver Beats, and Beatals.

There is no authoritative account of how the search reached its end: the *a*, of course, that turns "Beetles" from a mere insect into "Beatles," an insect with rhythm. The Buddy Holly allusion is there in any case, and so is the beat. When did the final *a* version fall into place? Hard to say exactly, but the first time we see them referred to as the "Beatles" was sometime before August 1960.

In May 1960, the foursome—the Silver Beetles this week—left Liverpool on a nine-day tour ("a musical and logistical fiasco," writes Jonathan Gould, the cultural historian and author of the impressive Beatles history *Can't Buy Me Love*) of a handful of provincial towns in central and northern Scotland. They were to accompany a Liverpool shipwright named John Askew; because of his repertoire of romantic ballads, his stage name was Johnny Gentle. A drummer came along too, a Liverpool bottle-factory worker named Tommy Moore, a good deal older than the members of the Silver Beetles.

As Johnny Gentle recalled, Paul was a more capable musician than his bandmates. "He just seemed to know what I was getting over. He

In Liverpool, the music world is tight. The fellow at right with the smile and cuppa is Rory Storm, who fronts his own band, the Hurricanes, and will soon involuntarily cede his drummer, Ringo Starr, to the Beatles. "I went out for a time with Rory's sister Iris, a dancer," Paul remembers in *The Beatles Anthology*. The late-night scene is just cups of tea and card games and chatting.

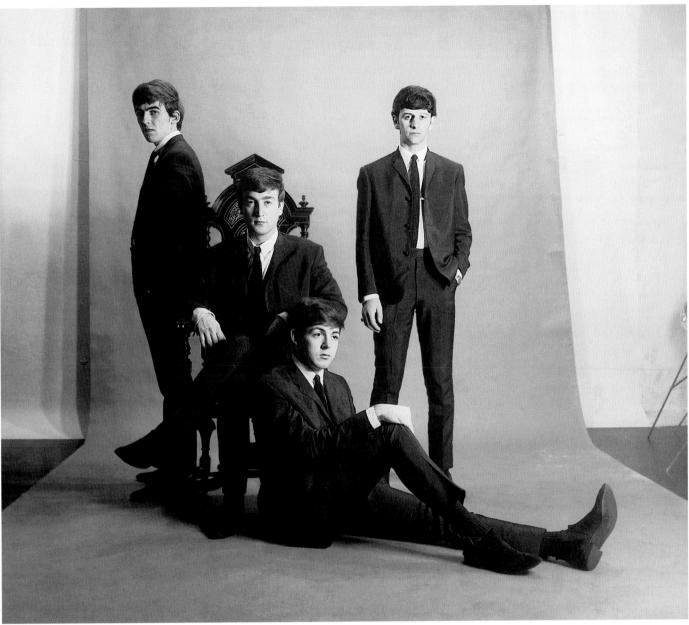

was one step ahead of John in that sense." The entire band, said Gentle, was unaccountably self-confident. They had no drummer and "they had a bass player"—Sutcliffe—"that was fairly useless . . . but they had a belief that they were going to make it."

On May 23, as they drove through the wilds of far northeastern Scotland to the next gig, in Fraserburgh, Johnny Gentle drove their van head-on into another car. Tommy Moore, sitting in the rear, was hurled forward against the front seat, breaking a number of teeth. They brought him to the nearest hospital, and he had barely been anesthetized and put to bed when a breathless Lennon was in the doorway shouting, "Come on then, Tommy! You can't just lie

here. We've got a gig to play!" Lennon pulled the groggy drummer out of his hospital bed while a nurse wrapped his jaw. Bandaged and well doped up, Tommy Moore managed to play the remaining shows. Back in Liverpool, he immediately left the band. A few days later, John went by Moore's house to beg him to return. But before he'd as much as rung the doorbell, Moore's girlfriend leaned out of an upstairs window and yelled at John, "You can go and piss off! He's not playing with you anymore!"

George later summed up the Scotland misadventure: "We were playing in Nowheresville to nobodies. Our shoes were full of holes, and our trousers were a mess . . . The band was horrible, an embarrassment."

Astrid Kirchherr, a photographer in Hamburg, was influential in the earliest days. She made these portraits and later recalled to LIFE: "Yes, I gave Stuart the haircut first—John made fun of it. But soon he wanted one too, and so did the others. The same haircut or not, each of them was strongly an individual. I could tell right away. When it all took off in England, well, nobody could expect that sort of thing. But I did always feel that each one of them was going to succeed."

Two and a half months after the Scotland debacle, Allan Williams, a Liverpool coffee shop owner recently bitten by the showbiz bug, talked the band into letting him represent them as their manager. Hearing that there was an active rock scene in Hamburg, Germany, he went to reconnoiter and found that English bands were indeed a hot commodity there. After negotiating with Bruno Koschmider, the peg-legged, gruffly Teutonic proprietor of the Kaiserkeller, a club in the heart of St. Pauli, Hamburg's world-famous district of iniquity, the deal was made. The Beatles—they'd decided to stick with the name—were to get £15 a week each, more than an adult with a solid, if modest, job—Mr. McCartney senior, for instance.

There was one thing missing: a drummer. No one knew of any available. Not Tommy Moore, certainly. Someone suddenly remembered 19-year-old Pete Best, whose mother ran the Casbah, one of the Quarry Men's venues. She had bought her son a drum kit a year before and he was fond of bashing on it. Paul

As far as the core of the band—John and Paul—they have never been tighter than at this moment: writing together, playing better every day, feeding off each other. The same can be said of the whole band, as John later confirms: "We were really hot musically. We were performers then and what we generated . . . was fantastic—there was nobody to touch us in Britain." Above: At the Cavern in 1963. Right: At the Cavern on February 19, 1963, three days before "Please Please Me" reaches No. 1 on the *New Musical Express* chart.

and John went to hear him at the Casbah. He couldn't play. The two Beatles looked at each other and shrugged. At least the kid was good-looking.

Seeking ways to think about the Beatles' story in mythological terms, Jonathan Gould borrows a concept from Joseph Campbell's magnum opus, *The Hero with a Thousand Faces:* the "monomyth." As Gould explains, "The hallmark of the monomyth is the theme of a journey to a strange and distant land, in the course of which a young man is tested by his encounters with various benevolent and malevolent forces, and from which the hero returns, sometimes in triumph, sometimes in flight, but either way transformed by the experience, and possessed of some new form of strength or knowledge that has the power to change the world."

The five Beatles—three veterans, two rookies—left for Hamburg on August 16, 1960, in Allan Williams's van. "I drove them to Hamburg," Williams said, "because they were that broke."

In 1960, Hamburg was the German Federal Republic's booming commercial center, its population 1.8 million. It was a maritime power as well, Germany's leading port, bisected by the 724-mile-long Elbe River, 60 miles from the North Sea. The city is highly Anglophone and Anglophile, which partly explains Hamburg's hunger for English rock 'n' roll. During the Beatles' first visit, the large number of other English bands there included Derry and the Seniors, Kingsize Taylor and the Dominoes, Vince Taylor and the Playboys, featuring Tony Sheridan, and Rory Storm and the Hurricanes, whose drummer, an affable little Liverpudlian named Richard Starkey, began palling around with the Beatles.

Allan Williams and his passengers headed straight for an infamous destination: the ancient St. Pauli neighborhood, since Bismarck's day transmogrified into the largest, most notorious center of sin in all of Europe. Through the quarter runs the equally notorious street the Reeperbahn and its offshoot Grosse Freiheit ("Great Freedom"), both lined, Gould writes, "with a garish array of neon-lit nightclubs, cafes, restaurants, cinemas, dance halls,

cabarets, strip joints, peep shows, gay bars, sex shops, flophouses and brothels where, side by side with more seemly types of entertainment every type of erotic activity, from mere titillation to the most bizarre forms of copulation, could be seen or had for a price."

To the Beatles' consternation, there was a change in the program. Bruno Koschmider had switched them from the Kaiserkeller to another of his properties, the second-string Indra, a cramped former strip joint on Grosse Freiheit. And they were aghast when he took them to their living quarters on nearby Paul Roosen-Strasse: two smelly rooms behind the screen of a decaying porn cinema, the Bambi Kino, yet another Koschmider holding. There were no windows, there were no toilets, and there was nowhere to put their clothes.

Most of the music in St. Pauli was second-rate Dixieland. Koschmider wanted loud rock 'n' roll that would pull in a young, free-spending clientele. (His letterhead read: *Kaiserkeller, ein Tanzpalast der Jugend*"—Kaiserkeller, a dance palace for youth.)

The Beatles, atypically, played too sedately to fit the game plan. Koschmider stood in the rear of the Indra, bellowing *"Mach Schau!"*— literally "Make show!" or in modern vernacular, "Get down!" Picking it up quickly, Paul, John and George were soon hollering *"Mach Schau!"* at one another onstage.

The band was dismayed, too, to discover the number of hours they would be expected to play: 24 to 36 a week, as a minimum. It seemed impossible. Apart from the attendant exhaustion, their meager repertoire consisted of 15 two-minute songs. Their first attempted solution was to draw each one out to epic lengths (Ray Charles's "What'd I Say" was perfect for this), strumming the same three-chord sequence for 15 minutes. But this quickly got to be tiresome. The only answer was to expand their repertoire, pillaging LPs, singles and the songs of their fellow Kaiserkeller and Indra rockers. In very little time, they developed a deep, respectable repertoire of rock 'n' roll, rhythm and blues, blues and even country. "They'd built up a two-or-three-hour show's worth of their own stamping rhythm, good and loud," writes Gould.

So now it starts, with good humor and adult japery at first, then with truly frightening intensity: Beatlemania. There are all the claims out there that Sinatra- or Elvis- or Madonna- or NKOTB- or One Direction-mania was (or were) worse or bigger or more dangerous, but what does it matter? What profit is there in measuring pop mania quantitatively or qualitatively? Beatlemania was nutty enough and relatively prolonged—that much we can agree on. England, certainly, had never seen anything like it (nor has it since), and in the postwar years, it was just what the Brits needed: a bit of kick-out-the-jams, kick-in-the-arse insanity. It started calmly enough, with young boys telling their barbers (when their mums were out of earshot), "It's okay. Let it tickle the ears." And then there were those sweet moments, early on, when Paul could actually commune with a fan (bottom) and sign both his first and last names. The photos here, just as the wave is building, cresting but not yet broken, are the visual definition of the phrase *the end of innocence.*

They still had a long way to go. Stu Sutcliffe's and Pete Best's incompetence hamstrung them. Best played very primitively, unimaginatively sticking to the basic snare drum, cymbal, bass drum combination, unless it was to play inevitably the same fill. Only one Beatle—Paul—was confidently on the path to professionalism. "Of the four," said George Martin, the Beatles' eventual producer, "Paul was the one most likely to be a professional musician, in the sense of learning the trade, learning about notation, harmony and counterpoint." This was the opinion, too, of Astrid Kirchherr, the young German photographer who became fascinated with the band and took a number of memorable photographs of them throughout Hamburg. When Kirchherr fell in love with Sutcliffe, her jilted boyfriend is said to have been admirably chivalrous. A graphics student and future musician named Klaus Voorman, he renewed his friendship with the Beatles five or so years later, going on to have

a decades-long relationship with the band members. In 1966, he drew the splendid cover of *Revolver*, and in 1969, playing bass, he was a member of John Lennon's Plastic Ono Band, along with Eric Clapton.

One of the group's most beneficial Hamburg contacts was an English rock 'n' roller named Tony Sheridan. The Beatles' contemporary but already a veteran trouper and recording artist, Sheridan was the best guitar player they had ever encountered, and a polished, if Elvis-derivative, vocalist. He was also rebellious and obnoxious enough to have worn out his welcome with so many British music businessmen that he had decamped for Germany. While the Beatles were playing the Kaiserkeller (they had been promoted from the Indra), Sheridan was at the Top Ten, a higher-class St. Pauli club. He immediately liked his inexperienced countrymen and appointed himself their tutor, expanding their repertoire further still, giving them

Said photographer Terry Spencer to LIFE, regarding the early days of fame in England: "I remember that, although they weren't at all conceited, they were quite self-conscious about their appearance. They used to sit in front of a long mirror—they always shared a dressing room—to do their hair and make themselves up. They used minimal makeup, just a little powder to offset the sweat." Results such as those above were precisely what John and Paul were aiming for in the Spencer photo at left.

guitar lessons and performing yet another service, turning them on to the amphetamine relative Preludin, a significant aid to playing marathon sets and providing enough energy to stay up indefinitely, club-hopping, chasing German girls and indulging in any number of illicit activities.

The phrase *sex and drugs and rock 'n' roll* may as well have been coined to express the Beatles' Hamburg existence. They involved themselves deeply in all three, sleeping with a tremendous number of both prostitutes and well-shod bourgeoisie, the latter especially entranced by these sweaty, scruffy, leather-clad English rockers. All of them contracted gonorrhea; in addition, Paul was hit with a paternity suit that followed him for decades. Stoked on Preludin, John might come onstage with a toilet seat around his neck, or take a nap midset under the piano, or scream at the audience, "Where are your tanks now, bastard krauts!" or *"Sieg Heil!"* (the latter illegal to utter in postwar Germany). According to McCartney biographer Chet Flippo, John "felt so immune on Preludin that he would with impunity kick in the face any hapless drunken German who wandered too near the stage and became too much of a pest."

The Beatles decided to mug a drunken clubgoer to pay back some money they owed. Paul and George begged off, but John and Pete Best stuck with the plan. They'd chosen a drunken sailor at the club; trailing him when he left, they threw him up against a gate. To their frightened surprise, the guy was tough. He pulled a gun, fired and missed. Amazed by his own courage, John charged. Then they ran. The sailor fired again, and they kept running, terrified.

John's antics notwithstanding, from modeling toilet seats to assault and attempted robbery, these adolescents (all but Lennon were under 20, Harrison a mere 17) accomplished something lasting, in which red-light Hamburg played a significant role:

"Apart from the other English musicians on the scene, no one in Hamburg knew them, and no one cared what they did," writes Gould. "This extended respite from the familiarity and reflexive debunkery of Liverpool, which blunted ambition as surely as it punctured pretension, granted the Beatles the license to be whoever they wanted to be."

Paul, who would for the duration of the band be perceived as the "nice" Beatle as well as the "cute" one, was toughening. It is also important to note: He never eschewed the path chosen in this period by the group (or dictated by John). He was in this entirely, feet-first. Hamburg didn't bug him, whether or not he was electing to roll a sailor. He and all of them felt that the Beatles were starting to happen, at least to a basic degree, and they were excited, juiced young men.

The Beatles made three Hamburg trips during this period. The first and second were more than three-month stays, from August 16 to December 5, 1960, and from March 24 to July 3, 1961; the third lasted eight weeks, from April 8 to June 2, 1962. The venue on the third trip was the relatively upscale Star-Club, where the Beatles got to rub elbows with their most famous headliner yet, the rockabilly icon Gene Vincent.

The crucial event of the German sojourns was the Beatles' first professional recording session, on June 22 and 23, for Hamburg-based Polydor Records. The session was not, in fact, the Beatles' but Tony Sheridan's—again, the Beatles' semi-mentor while abroad. The session's one release was credited to "Tony Sheridan and the Beat Brothers." The group backed Sheridan on seven songs in all, including two of their own. They were very much second fiddles.

It's amusing that the composer of "Strangers in the Night" and "Danke Schoen" produced the Beatles' first professionally made record. Here we had a master of easy-listening music riding herd over an undisciplined, instinctively mutinous bunch of rowdy rock 'n' rollers. The maestro under discussion is Bert Kaempfert, a Hamburg native who had successfully gone bicontinental, as much in demand in the U.S. as in Europe. He was a music man of many skills: songwriter (he had written "Strangers in the Night" not for Sinatra but for the 1966 Hollywood comedy *A Man Could Get Killed*—Sinatra's monster

hit reared its head later that year; and "Danke Schoen," which was the signature song of the sweet, harmless Wayne Newton, a fixture on '60s TV variety shows); bandleader ("Sweet Caroline," the Neil Diamond product now best known as the eighth-inning anthem of the world champion Boston Red Sox) and arranger (sentimental treacle including "Red Roses for a Blue Lady"—yikes).

Regardless of his bread-and-butter schlock, Kaempfert was entirely at home producing rock 'n' roll. He had already let it be known that the Beatles did not impress him. Why, then, did he choose them to accompany Tony Sheridan? The only answer that presents itself is that Kaempfert surmised that four Reeperbahn toughs would make the best available fit with another such outlaw.

The centerpiece of the Kaempfert/Sheridan/Beat Brothers session was "My Bonnie," one of the few indications of how the Beatles sounded in these very early days. "My Bonnie" is Sheridan's retooling of the traditional waltz "My Bonnie Lies over the Ocean." After 16 measures of the original melody, meter (waltz time) and tempo (slow), singer and band burst into high-speed rock. After the rest of Sheridan's songs had gone to tape, the Beatles recorded two: the Tin Pan Alley standard "Ain't She Sweet," sung by Lennon, and "Cry for a Shadow," an instrumental written by Lennon and Harrison, who plays a clumsy, amateurish solo. George plays all of his early solos on one string, making no attempt at the multistring harmonies that make a guitar solo, and guitar playing in general, interesting.

The weakest link is Pete Best, who plays the same unimaginative beat throughout, and shakily. His bass drum hits a constant, mentally deadening, four beats per measure—*thump, thump, thump, thump*—while an equally unchanging snare drum (always snare drum) fill, is chucked in every few measures. John Lennon's rhythm guitar is barely audible. Only one band member plays with dexterity and intelligence—McCartney, all the more remarkably, given the few months that had elapsed since he had somewhat reluctantly taken on bass guitar duties from the departed Sutcliffe. The painter had quit

after a raging fistfight with McCartney, who'd finally had enough of Sutcliffe's inept playing. The band was paring, and improving. A listener in Hamburg might have guessed that, if the Beatles ever made it big, Pete Best would not be with them.

(A slight, fun but important footnote in passing, albeit one well known to Beatles fans and alluded to briefly in a caption just a few pages back: Before Stu Sutcliffe left the group, Astrid Kirchherr inspired what would soon become a vital feature of the Beatles' evolving appearance. During the band's second Hamburg stay, Kirchherr styled Sutcliffe's hair into what was known as a *Pilzenkopf,* or "mushroom head": a haircut popular among German students, in which the front hung down to just above the eyes. John, Paul and George scrutinized Stu's *Pilzenkopf* curiously. But no one took any steps until John and Paul, funded by a birthday gift of £100 from John's aunt Mimi, made a first visit to Paris. They looked up the only person they knew, Astrid's Hamburg friend Jurgen Vollmer. Jurgen was wearing a first-rate *Pilzenkopf,* and the time seemed right—John and Paul said they wanted mushroom heads as well. Eventually, George wanted one too. Astrid complied. So it was that two young Germans midwifed the Beatles haircut, the tonsorial style that would soon provoke thousands of mindless comments by American journalists.)

The Polydor recordings are the first of many in which McCartney showed talent and skill beyond that of his bandmates. His almost effortless excellence in Hamburg was a portent of the future, in which McCartney was recognized for decades as rock's finest bass player—"probably the best bass guitar player there is," in the opinion of perhaps the best-qualified judge, the group's future producer, George Martin.

"My Bonnie" is held in high esteem by most of the critics and Beatles historians who have commented on it. Howard Sounes, the author of a 600-page McCartney biography, pronounces the song a "rave-up." Another McCartney biographer, James Kaplan, turns up the enthusiasm dial a notch. "My Bonnie," he writes, is "a rocking rave up."

On June 26, 1963, Paul and John finish a concert in Newcastle upon Tyne (they're touring with Roy Orbison and Gerry and the Pacemakers), and on the bus they start writing "She Loves You." They finish it later that night at the hotel in Newcastle. It is different in that it is in the third person, not the first, and much later Lennon will credit that to his partner. "It was Paul's idea: instead of singing 'I love you' again, we'd have a third party. That kind of little detail is still in his work. He will write a story about someone. I'm more inclined to write about myself." The two take the song and play it on acoustic guitars for Paul's father: "We went into the living room [and said] 'Dad, listen to this. What do you think?' And he said 'That's very nice, son, but isn't there enough of these Americanisms around? Couldn't you sing 'She loves you, yes, yes, yes!' At which point we collapsed in a heap and said 'No, Dad, you don't quite get it!'" In the top photo, the songwriters record the song at Abbey Road studio, and in the bottom picture, part of the reaction to it—and all that is now "Beatles"—is enacted at the Pavilion dance hall on November 4, 1963. "She Loves You" is the biggest song of 1963 in the U.K. and one of the five straight No. 1 singles that help the Beatles put a stranglehold on the top spot of the American charts in '64.

A more authoritative if hardly unbiased source begs to differ. "It's just Tony Sheridan singing, with us banging in the background. It's terrible. It could be anybody." John Lennon has just weighed in from more than 40 years ago. "My Bonnie," and, by extension, his band's performances throughout the Hamburg session, do not pass muster with the "smart" Beatle.

One might ask iconoclastically, "Were the Beatles in Hamburg any good?" With the sole recorded evidence seven songs, with only two of these by the Beatles alone and without any way to see their performances, it's impossible to make a reliable judgment. James Kaplan writes: "Hamburg, [the Beatles'] crucible, turned them from a larking bunch of amateurs into a real rock and roll band." If anything distinguished the Beatles' music at this point in their career, the small amount of evidence points to a raw spontaneity: backup singer Paul's hyena whoops and screams on "My Bonnie," John's raspy vocals and the band's generally unruly, slapdash sound, something like a 20-years-early Sex Pistols. Live, the Beatles' chief attractions were extramusical: their delight in flouting convention, for instance, and doing it again and again. Or their effortless hilarity—this would be John, who could make an audience laugh at the insults he rained down on it. At the London Palladium in October 1963, John mocked the audience, already noisily laughing, with his awful spastic routine and shouted "Shut up!" which only made them laugh harder.

And there was one last ace in the hole . . .

"They had this *charm*," said the man who would become their producer, early label head and close collaborator, George Martin. "They had the quality that when you were with them, you felt richer for being with them and when they left the room, you felt diminished . . . And I thought to myself: *If they have that effect on me, they're going to have that effect on other people on the stage.* So I signed them."

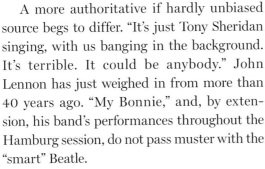

The mania has spread beyond England: In France, Denmark, Holland (here, in Hillegom), the Beatles are the biggest things, with language barriers no deterrent. Even Ringo's brief illness doesn't stop them (that's Jimmie Nicol up there on drums).

Much of the early part of this narrative deals with the Beatles as a whole, rather than with Paul alone. McCartney was not far, however, from having his own musical identity. Forming himself, he was simultaneously being formed by the band (as was each of his mates), but within a very few years, Paul would be recognizably himself: the disarming lead vocalist on his 1963 composition "All My Loving" and the composer/singer, onstage alone, of the most-covered song ever, "Yesterday," which Paul wrote in 1965.

The formation continues.

The second German sojourn over, home they came, anxious to quickly reestablish themselves after their three-month absence.

If the band remained shaky in some areas, there were others in which they were well-grounded indeed. Their devotion to the visceral sound of rock 'n' roll's early geniuses, for one: Chuck Berry, Little Richard, Buddy Holly (from whose band, as we've seen, the Beatles took inspiration for their name), Jerry Lee Lewis and others. (In their first years, the Beatles sought inspiration—material, too—in the music of rock 'n' roll's pioneers and were even seen by some as an "oldies" band.) Bob Wooler, the Cavern Club's DJ, Beatles friend and frequent contributor to the opinionated fanzine *Mersey Beat*, wrote perceptively about the Beatles' popularity, which by the end of 1961 was rising almost daily on Merseyside. "I think the Beatles are No. 1 because they resurrected original style rock 'n' roll," Wooler wrote. "They hit the scene when it had been emasculated by figures like Cliff Richard and sounds like those electronic wonders, the Shadows and their many imitators. Gone was the drive that inflamed the emotions. The Beatles, therefore, exploded on a jaded scene. And to those people on the verge of quitting teendom—those who had experienced during their most impressionable years the impact of rhythm & blues music (raw rock 'n' roll)—this was an experience, a process of regaining and reliving a style of sounds . . . Here again, in the Beatles, was the stuff that screams are made of. Here was the excitement—both physical and aural—that symbolized the rebellion of youth in the ennuied mid-1950s . . . Rugged yet romantic, appealing to both sexes. With calculated naiveté and an ingenious, throwaway approach to their music . . . Reviving interest in, and commanding enthusiasm for, numbers which descended the charts way back."

The Beatles' rise into the Merseyside firmament took place largely in a single location. This was the Cavern Club, in the cellar of an old fruit-and-vegetable warehouse on Mathew Street. Between February 1961 and August 1963, the Beatles played 290 sets here. The Cavern's owner since 1960, an accountant named Ray McFall, had instituted a two-shows-per-day policy, one at lunchtime, the other in the evening. The latter could be, and often was, pandemonium, especially when the Beatles played to their mushrooming crowd.

"Day or night," writes Jonathan Gould, "the Beatles' performances were marked by their willful disregard for the niceties of a polished presentation." In other words, they went wild—and at night-time they went a good deal wilder. At the group's first evening show in February 1961, their friend and fellow Liverpool rocker Gerry Marsden, front man for Gerry and the Pacemakers, came down to the Cavern to take it all in. "I couldn't believe how good they were," Marsden said. "The energy, the way they shaped up to the microphone together, you know—Paul the left-handed bass player, John standing there, couldn't give a s——, the attitude of the man. I thought, *They'll be the first band out of Liverpool to make it.*"

An unlikely person was shortly to make that his business for the rest of his life.

There are several versions of what will be known as the "iconic" Beatles "jump photo" made on March 25, 1963, at Allerton Golf Course in Liverpool by photographer Dezo Hoffman—and even today you can take your pick of a favorite. This is ours. Today, a silhouette, with the bandmates rearranged, is the representative image for the Las Vegas Cirque de Soleil show *Love,* based on Beatles music.

"Brian was a beautiful guy . . . an intuitive, theatrical guy, and he knew we had something. He presented us well." —John Lennon

"[Brian] tried everywhere and everyone turned him down. And [the Beatles] . . . thought they were never going to make it. Brian had this unswerving conviction that they were great and that they were going to make it and I think without that conviction—without that sincerity, I don't think that I would have brought them down from Liverpool to listen to them. And I think it's a tribute to him." —George Martin

"If anyone was the Fifth Beatle, it was Brian." —Paul McCartney

Born and raised in Liverpool's Jewish community, scion of a wealthy mercantile family, Brian Epstein, while still in his early twenties, established a chain of stores (NEMS, for North End Music Stores), largely specializing in records. Brian and his brother, Clive, built their merchandising network into one of the largest record retailers in northern England.

Brian's substantial achievements notwithstanding, he was dissatisfied with life and longed for more stimulating work than selling records. He had artistic ambitions that he himself had thwarted. At 22, he had enrolled in the top-notch Royal Academy of Dramatic Art in London. Although his teachers had declared him "a really promising student," he'd dropped out, worried about his prospects as a professional actor.

"There was a sort of wistfulness about him," said a fellow actor. "He wanted to belong to what he perceived as a charmed circle. He was obviously bored to death with . . . business and he thought we were terribly lucky people, that we inhabited a magic world which he wanted to become a part of." Her comments accurately point out the conventionally raised, conventionally employed young Epstein's need to cultivate

Paul is poised in late 1963. He has the band he dreamed of. He is confident enough, while harboring some of his innate—and useful—insecurity. Life is going well and he is not thinking that any of this is coming to an end anytime soon.

his imagination, to have the courage to break middle-class rules and to live in a community whose members shared his dreams.

In October 1961, Brian later recalled, a larger-than-usual number of teenage kids started coming into NEMS's Whitechapel store, which he managed, asking for a record called "My Bonnie." To handle a growing demand, said Epstein, he ordered several hundred copies. This doesn't jibe with Paul's memory that the song "did nothing over here." Whether Epstein's recollection was accurate, or something else had prompted him—such as the heavy coverage of the Beatles in *Mersey Beat* and the other local music magazines he carried in his store—he decided to have a look.

So at lunchtime on November 9, 1961, Brian and his assistant Alistair Taylor (who would later work for the Beatles) walked the few blocks from the Whitechapel store to the Cavern Club, where the band was playing the noon show.

Epstein later remembered vividly his first viewing of them, at one of the club's midday shows: "I had never seen anything like the Beatles on *any* stage. They smoked as they played and they talked and pretended to hit one another. They turned their backs on the audience and shouted at them and laughed at private jokes. Everything about the Beatles was right for me. Their kind of attitude toward life, and their humor, and their own personal way of behaving—it was all just what I wanted." Taylor remembered that "the music was so loud, we couldn't hear ourselves think. They were deafening. And so unprofessional—laughing with the girls, smoking onstage and sipping from Cokes during their act. But absolutely magic! The vibe they generated was just unbelievable."

After the Beatles' set, Epstein and Taylor squeezed into the Cavern's virtual closet of a dressing room so that Brian could introduce himself, then he and Taylor headed back to the store. On the way, Epstein asked Taylor what he thought about the Beatles. Taylor equivocated. "I think they're tremendous!" Brian almost shouted. He grabbed Taylor's arm. "Do you think I should manage them?"

Epstein didn't even like rock 'n' roll. A classical music lover, he considered rock barbaric. What, with just one look, made him a helpless advocate? Very likely his realization, or hope, that with their enviable freedom from the bourgeois propriety with which he had been raised, the Beatles might lead him out of his deadly dull salesman's life. "[Epstein] serendipitously [found] in the Beatles," writes Gould, "the perfect vehicle for all of his unformed and unrealized creative aspirations."

"Everything about the Beatles was right for me," Epstein said in 1964. "Their kind of attitude toward life, and their humor, and their own personal way of behaving—it was all just what I wanted. They represented the direct, unselfconscious, good-natured, uninhibited human relationships which I hadn't found and had wanted and felt deprived of. And my own sense of inferiority evaporated with the Beatles because I knew I could help them and that they wanted me to help them, and trusted me to help them."

Aside from his fascination with their humor, joie de vivre and apparently inexhaustible energy, there was a second reason for Brian Epstein's interest in the Beatles: They were four attractive young men, and he was gay.

Epstein's homosexuality was revealed only after his sadly premature death at 32. While he lived, neither he nor his family nor friends disclosed his "secret." Which is easy to understand—in Britain, homosexuality didn't merely carry the stigma that it did in the United States, but until the Sexual Offenses Act of 1967, it was illegal. Gay men in midcentury England, in other words, lived under legal conditions identical to those of the 19th century and earlier.

Did Epstein come on to any of the Beatles? Probably, although it's hard to know for sure. Pete Best and John Lennon both claimed that Epstein, shyly and self-effacingly, approached each of them—Best in 1962, Lennon a year later. It has long been bruited, moreover, that Epstein and Lennon had a quick affair while on a Spanish vacation together in 1963. It is often said that Lennon wrote the 1965 Beatles song "You've Got to Hide Your Love Away" for the closeted Epstein. Given Epstein's active homosexuality, a number of writers over the years have been unable to resist arguing that sexuality alone is what drove Epstein toward the Beatles. Which is to believe that the other

motives we have named, from boredom with a salesman's lot to a desire to take control of his life, played no part. To argue that Epstein and the Beatles' relationship was rooted solely in Epstein's homosexuality—the line taken by the biographer Albert Goldman in his 1988 *The Lives of John Lennon* and elsewhere—is a gross simplification of a multifaceted relationship.

On December 3, 1961, three weeks after Brian's revelation at the Cavern, he invited the Beatles to his office at the Whitechapel store and offered to manage them. Music business neophytes, they were wary. What they really needed, they said, was a record contract. "Well," said Epstein, with a confidence that he had formerly lacked outside the world of commerce. "I think I can handle that." In a generous gesture, he told them that he wouldn't sign a contract with them until he'd firmly hooked them up with a record label. The usual dickering about percentages ensued, with Epstein holding to 25 percent. Perhaps a bit jittery, he announced, "That'll do, now I'll be your manager."

Was this the right step for them, the right person? Brian Epstein, they were aware, probably knew less about the music business than they did. The Beatles weren't yet ready to celebrate; in fact, they were more than a bit queasy. It was Paul who, camouflaging his doubts, approached the new manager, telling Epstein that he hoped the Beatles were going to succeed and adding: "But I'll tell you now, Mr. Epstein, I'm going to be a star anyway."

We go on for a little bit about Brian Epstein because, it can be claimed, no one else would be more important than he to whom each of them would become (Paul's confidence, mock or forthright, notwithstanding). Of course, in the beginning, no one would have bet that way.

Epstein's promise to the Beatles that he would get them a recording contract was looking, for a time, like nothing but bravado. Crisscrossing London for months, a tape canister under his arm, Epstein had gotten a

The Ed Sullivan Show buildup (opposite) and big moment (above). Seventy-three million are watching. They deliver five songs live: "All My Loving," "Till There Was You," "She Loves You," "I Saw Her Standing There," "I Want to Hold Your Hand." That—and the rest—is history. "A lot of fathers did turn it off," says Paul later. "But a lot of mothers and children made them keep it on." (By the way, those are Walter Cronkite's daughters in the middle photo, right.)

thumbs-down from every record label he knew of. Decca, one of Britain's two largest record companies (the other was EMI), had given Epstein's group not one, but two listens, after which the label's A&R head said, "Not to mince words, Mr. Epstein, but we don't like your boys' sound." The Beatles were starting to get antsy and wonder if they were going to get any offer at all. "It's very hard to guess what would have happened if they'd gone unsigned," said George Martin, who was then the head of the EMI subsidiary Parlophone. "Possibly they would just have broken up and never have been heard of again."

A series of coincidences had brought Epstein to Parlophone, the only label in London he had not visited, no doubt because of its obscurity (Martin liked to call it "the poor relation" of the EMI family).

It was Martin into whose office Brian Epstein was ushered one April day in 1962. At 36, Martin was tall, slender and disarmingly handsome, his blond hair periodically flopping down over his forehead, with a strong nose and a plummy Oxbridge accent. What puzzled and attracted Epstein was that with all of these aristocratic appurtenances, Martin's manner was the opposite of coldly upper class; rather, he had a friendly gleam in his blue eyes and a ready, sympathetic smile.

If Martin was free of upper-class arrogance, it's because he wasn't upper class. Born in 1926 in Drayton Park, north London, he spent his earliest years in a decaying two-room flat with no electricity and no bathroom. George's father was a carpenter whom the Depression reduced to selling newspapers.

(Those interested in questions of class may wonder: Was Martin's self-transformation from plebeian to patrician the effort of a social climber, as Paul was sometimes accused of being? It is more likely that Martin's upward ascent was the effort of a poor man of ambition to avoid victimization by England's notoriously rigid social system. Upper-class manners can never be underestimated as an aid to success, especially in the business world; a polished and smooth comportment can be the difference between a millionaire and an underdressed man selling newspapers in the cold. It is interesting in the context of this story, since the Liverpudlian Beatles, each of whom was a disrespectful wag when the moment called for it, did so much to alter the fundamental structure.)

When he was only six, George Martin's parents saved to buy a piano and lessons for him. When the lessons ended unexpectedly, the boy taught himself. He won a scholarship to a Jesuit grammar school, after which he served in the wartime navy. He used his veteran's grant to attend the world-class Guildhall School of Music & Drama, where he studied piano and oboe. He wasn't a very good oboist; at his exam, he recalled, "that oboe became like a live eel in my hands."

Martin accepted that he was never going to be a professional performer. Casting about for work, he was hired in 1950 as assistant to the head of Parlophone. When his boss retired in 1955, Martin, only 29, became the label's new chief.

Before long, almost everyone involved with Martin became aware of his remarkable range of talents: corporate executive, record producer, recording engineer, classically trained pianist, composer, arranger for any size of ensemble, acoustician and talent scout. Addressing his versatility with characteristic modesty, Martin said, "I am a jack-of-all-trades, and master of none, and it is fortunate for me that I have found a line of business which accepts versatility rather than genius."

Although his passion was music, Martin became known as the producer of some of the great comedy records of the '50s—of any decade: albums with Peter Sellers and Spike Milligan of *The Goon Show,* a major cultural force; *Beyond the Fringe* (Jonathan Miller, Dudley Moore, Peter Cook and Alan Bennett); and Flanders and Swann. Martin's industry nickname was "the comedy king," with which he was not entirely happy; as much as he loved working with as great a comic as Sellers, Martin had remained a musician first. "Music was pretty much my whole life," he writes in *All You Need Is Ears,* his 2002 memoir, and he was beginning to feel uncomfortably distant from his native milieu. It was at this point that he started listening to lots of demos and coined a motto for himself: Will listen to anything.

Everyone knew there was a movie in the making. No one was predicting it would be terrific and funny and just as vibrant as the whole Beatles thing itself. *A Hard Day's Night*'s signature image is opposite, and on this page are intimate, behind-the-scenes shots, and then the big opening night at the London Pavilion on July 6, 1964. (On the train, top left, Paul is hamming it up next to a young blonde model named Pattie Boyd—the future Mrs. George Harrison and, later, Mrs. Eric Clapton.)

BERT CANN

ULF KRUGER/K&K/REDFERNS/GETTY

DAVID HORN/MAGNUM (2)

MAX SCHELER/K&K/REDFERNS/GETTY

UNITED ARTISTS/MOVIE STILL ARCHIVES

HARRY MYERS/REX USA

Martin listened to everything—including the demo that Brian Epstein, "a well-spoken, smartly turned out, engagingly amiable, 'clean' young man," in Martin's eyes, was urgently touting to him. "What I didn't realize at the time," says Martin in *All You Need*, "was that he was in London for his final, desperate attempt to get someone interested in his group, the Beatles . . . He gave me a big 'hype,' about this marvelous group who were doing such great things in Liverpool. He told me how everybody up there thought they were the bee's knees."

Epstein played the disc, "and I first heard the sound of the Beatles," remembered Martin. He was by no means blown away. He could see why the group had been turned down all over town. There were some moldy vaudeville-type tunes—what were they doing there? wondered Martin, taken aback—Fats Waller's "Your Feet's Too Big" and the extremely corny "Besame Mucho," which Paul had been singing for years. Moreover, the group's self-written songs, including "Love Me Do," were "very mediocre." Yet something kept Martin from dismissing Epstein's protégés. "There was an unusual quality of sound," recalled the record man, "a certain roughness that I hadn't encountered before . . . There was something tangible that made me want to hear more."

So on June 6, the Beatles turned up at Abbey Road Studios for a recording test: putting a song onto tape and judging the result. Martin was smitten by the band members even as they introduced themselves—the label chief recalled his reaction as "love at first sight . . . They were just great people to be with."

His delight in their personalities notwithstanding, Martin was as unimpressed as before about their music. He was "quite certain," he recalled, "that their songwriting ability had no saleable future." To introduce them to the activity of producing, and thereby shaping a song, Martin brought them into the control booth, where they listened to their songs in high-quality audio, after which Martin asked them if there was anything they didn't like. "I don't like your tie," George Harrison said. Martin cracked up, thinking that maybe he should sign the Beatles just for their wit, which reminded him of his old Goons charges Sellers and Milligan

(not surprisingly, back in its mid-'50s heyday, *The Goon Show* was devoured and memorized by the Liverpool teenager John Lennon). In any case, having fallen for these eccentric provincials, Martin decided that none of his reservations about their music really mattered.

We go on more than a little bit here about George Martin because, if Paul's assessment was incorrect and Epstein wasn't the Fifth Beatle, Martin certainly was—crucial in all that would follow. Moreover, he and McCartney, in particular, would never part. He would always be called back in to help with Paul's solo efforts, and it is somewhere between poignant and piquant that the lion's share of songs on the newest album, *New*, are produced—to wonderful effect—by Martin's son Giles.

At the June 6, 1962, "test," Martin became aware of, and accepted, a subtle, quiet Beatles innovation that would not be without impact. When he had first met them, Martin later recalled, "there was no obvious leader . . . I went home wondering which one of them was going to be the star." In the England of the early '60s (in America too, though less emphatically), stars were solo artists, like the then-hot singers Cliff Richard and Tommy Steele. "I couldn't imagine a group being successful as a group," said Martin: One of the members would inevitably turn out to be a better singer than the others. "Whoever that was would be the one, and the rest would become like Cliff Richard's backing group, the Shadows." As to how this dynamic would inevitably come to define the Beatles, Martin admitted: "I was quite wrong."

At first Martin felt that Paul had "a sweeter voice, John's had more character and George was generally not so good." Paul should be the leader, Martin thought. But on further consideration, Martin realized that if he designated Paul the leader, "I would be changing the nature of the group. Why do that? Why not keep them as they were?" It went against convention, but so what? Martin had already done his share of experimenting. And so the Beatles initiated a practice that stuck. Instead of Gerry and the Pacemakers, Freddie & the Dreamers,

The Beatles change the game time and again. No rock act had played a stadium concert before, but the Beatles are the Beatles, and so on August 15, 1965, they perform at Shea Stadium in Queens, New York City, before more than 55,000 fans, 21 of whom hear a note of the music played. (The songs, delivered in about half an hour, were: "Twist and Shout," "She's a Woman," "I Feel Fine," "Dizzy Miss Lizzy," "Ticket to Ride," "Everybody's Trying to Be My Baby," "Can't Buy Me Love," "Baby's in Black," "Act Naturally," "A Hard Day's Night," "Help!" and "I'm Down"—equal parts John and Paul, a little Ringo, a shortchanged George, four cover songs out of 12, a finale of tremendous recent rockers by John and then Paul. Paul on John's song: "From something he said later, I think 'Help!' reflected John's state of mind. He was feeling a bit constricted by the Beatle thing.") The young woman opposite in the floral dress professes her allegiance this night with a picture. Paul remembered later that, since the entire affair was unprecedented and truly scary, it was good to be playing alongside John: "John was having a good time at Shea. He was into his comedy, which was great. That was one of the great things about John. If there was ever one of those tense shows, which this undoubtedly was (you can't play in front of that many people for the first time and not be tense), his comedy routines would always come out . . . He kept us jolly."

Top: Paul and George check up on the King, circa 1965. Bottom: In a more major moment that year, the Beatles pose with their Member of the British Empire medals, which had been bestowed by Queen Elizabeth II, who was at least a little clueless, asking Ringo when he approached, "You started the group, did you?" He helped her with the chronology, then she asked how long the band had been together. Paul joined him in explaining that they had been together 40 years "and it don't seem a day too much." Remembered Ringo: "She had this strange, quizzical look on her face, like either she wanted to laugh or she was thinking, 'Off with their heads!'" There were indeed grumbles about the Beatles getting the nod, and they probably did toke a little in the loo, but Paul was probably most clear-eyed later about what it was all really about: "There was only one fella who said, 'I want your autograph for my daughter. I don't know what she sees in you.' Most other people were pleased about us getting the award . . . In some ways we'd become super salesmen for Britain." On the following pages are three more from 1965 and '66, clockwise from top left: During a break in the filming of *Help!* at Cliveden House in Buckinghamshire; Paul in London inadvertently helping British threads and automotives; relaxing with a cigarette, ubiquitous in the band.

Billy J. Kramer & the Dakotas (or, for that matter, Johnny & the Moondogs) or, stateside, Shep and the Limelites, Dion and the Belmonts or Smokey Robinson & the Miracles, you had the Rolling Stones—not Mick Jagger and the Rolling Stones, which would probably have been the choice five years earlier—the Hollies and the Beach Boys.

In the summer of '62, the Beatles played several times with their prospective drummer Ringo Starr, giving him a sustained testing. As mentioned, they'd met Ringo in Hamburg, where he was gigging with another Liverpool band, Rory Storm and the Hurricanes. They liked his playing. Born Richard Starkey, he had grown up in the Dingle, an all-but-slum district of Liverpool, which made him much more proletarian than his fellow blue-collar Beatles Paul and George. Bedridden for much of his childhood, Ritchie missed years of school, finally leaving at 15. He could read but hardly write. He worked as a pipe fitter, began playing drums at 17 or 18 and joined Rory Storm's band at age 20. Leaving his pipe fitter's job to become a full-time musician, he was shortly considered Liverpool's best drummer. (It must have been slim pickings among Liverpool drummers; there were a few things that Ringo did well—his tom-tom fills on "A Day in the Life," for instance—and his playing almost always sounded soulful, but overall, he was limited. Still, he has always possessed the drummer's essential skill: Unlike Pete Best, Ringo could keep a steady beat.)

Heading to Hamburg in late 1960 with the Hurricanes, Ringo befriended the Beatles, who liked his playing, and he asked them to keep him in mind for the future. After the recording test, the bell finally tolled for Pete Best. Following just one listen, George Martin was adamant that Best did not belong with the Beatles. Buttonholing Epstein, he whispered, "This drumming isn't good enough for what I want." Martin was merely confirming the three other Beatles' unhappiness with Best, and his remarks "were something in the nature of a last straw," Martin said. Epstein accepted the heavy's role, asking Best to his office and giving the shocked young man notice. The next several years were not happy ones for Best, to put it

mildly: At the height of the Beatles' popularity, he tried to kill himself.

And so they were four, and soon to be fab. In early September 1962, Martin summoned the Beatles to Abbey Road for the band's first two recording sessions—on the fourth and the 11th. The band, with Ringo aboard, recorded what the Beatles wanted to be the first single, "Love Me Do." Hearing Ringo for the first time, Martin was unmoved, considering the new drummer barely an improvement over the old. Scheduling a second session, Martin brought in a skilled studio drummer, who played throughout. Ringo stood and played tambourines, alternately furious and terrified that he was about to be fired. Perhaps to restore the new drummer's damaged confidence, Martin declared the version cut on the fourth, with Ringo playing, the keeper. Martin would spend a good deal of time and energy making up with Ringo, at one point calling him "probably . . . the finest rock drummer in the world today," which Martin, who has spent his life among great rock drummers, would no doubt be the first to call (in private) a white lie.

"Love Me Do" is probably in the bottom half of Lennon and McCartney tunes. It slogs along at a boring, barely medium tempo, its ultrasimple, three-chord harmonic structure equally uninteresting. The lyrics, too. The one nice touch is when the rhythm suddenly changes for the eight-bar instrumental midsong. But it was not a very convincing choice for a first release.

"Love Me Do" was a "modest, respectable debut," writes Jonathan Gould. Released in October 1962, it floated, more or less hidden, in the middle of the singles charts, finally topping out at No. 17—not high enough to command attention. "Well," Martin told a 1998 interviewer, "I knew we had to find a hit song and 'Love Me Do' wasn't it. I knew it straightaway. It got to No. 17, but it wasn't the blockbuster we were looking for." Lennon and McCartney had written a song entitled "Please Please Me" that Martin called "dreary." The two songwriters had meant to write a slow, impassioned, Roy Orbison–style torch song; to Martin's ears, it needed to be livened up. Taking the song back, the two writers

Today there are a million people who were at Candlestick Park in San Francisco on August 29, 1966, for the Beatles' last-ever concert (excluding the *Let It Be* rooftop session with no formal audience in London in 1969)—*a million people* who were there, or claim to have been. But in fact only 25,000 of 42,500 tickets were sold, for prices from $4.50 to $6.50. The abject nuttiness of Beatlemania was waning. John had said the band was more popular than Jesus Christ (hurting ticket sales immediately), and the '60s were moving on. So, now, were the lads—John and George in particular. They had had it with the road show. Nothing was announced in advance, but those on the inside knew what was going down. Can anything be perceived, these years later, in the Cheshire cat grins of Paul and George onstage that night (opposite) during the 11-song, 30-minute set? That's claiming too much. But Paul made sure the concert was recorded, and he and John brought a camera to the stage to take pictures of the crowd and the final moments onstage with their bandmates. Candlestick Park is scheduled to be torn down in 2014, and not long ago, before performing an outdoor concert before 65,000 (who had paid $75 to $105 each to attend), Paul suggested to San Francisco mayor Ed Lee that perhaps it would be cool for him to return and perform a last show at the 'Stick. "You know my agent," said Paul. "Why don't we follow up with him?" To be continued.

reworked it. This time, Martin thought it was great. Recording it, he said later, "worked beautifully." The soft-spoken Martin was almost never as audibly enthusiastic as when, the last notes ringing, he switched on the control-room intercom and said brightly, "Gentlemen, you've just made your first No. 1 record."

Predictions were flying through the air. We've just heard Martin's, and there was McCartney's "Mr. Epstein, either way I'm going to be a star" and, finally, Epstein's "I'm managing a band and they're going to be bigger than Elvis." For the Beatles in 1962, anything seemed possible. Just about anything *was* possible.

Peter Asher, who was then a figure on the English music scene as half of the duo Peter and Gordon and whose sister Jane, an actress, was Paul's famous paramour in the mid-1960s, once observed, "Paul's not easily cowed by people, and he counts on his very considerable charm, which works. He's a super-amiable, charming man—and very clever." Paul was and is all of this—and as the Beatles began to take off, his charm and confidence, coupled with Lennon's dogged determination, not to mention all that talent, would serve the band well.

"Please Please Me" was released on January 11, 1963, and less than six weeks later, George Martin's prediction hit the bull's-eye. Well, hit most of it. The British music business of the early '60s had no equivalent to the authoritative record charts in *Billboard*, America's music-biz bible. The situation in Britain was chaotic by comparison. There were at least four charts, one each in the periodicals *Disc, Melody Maker, New Musical Express* and *Record Mirror.* "Please Please Me" hit No. 1 on the first three charts; on *Record Mirror*'s, it ran out of petrol at No. 2. Which is why it was decided not to include the song in the self-explanatorily titled 2000 Beatles collection *1 (One)*. The Beatles had to wait until "From Me to You," released on April 11, rang all four charts' bells, to satisfy music-business hairsplitters.

"Please Please Me" was the Beatles' first U.S. single, coming out in February 1963, soon after its British release. But it didn't receive wide distribution or do well in the charts. In fact, the first

time most Americans heard the song wouldn't be till its *re*release in January 1964, after "She Loves You" and "I Want to Hold Your Hand" had already been pouring forth from stateside radios and record players. Like those other songs, "Please Please Me," with the descending, chiming guitar line that opens it, had a particular *sound* that made it immediately recognizable as springing from the same source.

The Beatles sounded different from every other band. Was it the "roughness" that George Martin heard when he listened to the group for the first time, on Brian Epstein's demo disc? Things *were* pretty messy. Notes that were supposed to be in unison landed apart. One guitar or another fell behind the beat. The drummer's fills were ragged. The lead singer's voice was certainly rough—but in a great way, especially when he sang "Come *on!*" You wanted to play the song over and over just for those "Come ons." Which Beatle was that, anyway?

And unlike a tune by a conventional early-'60s pop artiste—Steve Lawrence, Bobby Vinton, Andy Williams—in which the orchestra, the strings in particular, issues a penumbral sound, the individual instruments indistinguishable, melting into one another, in the Beatles' first songs, you could hear every note, including the wrong ones. Along with the unstoppable drive with which "Please Please Me" came hurtling into the room, there was indeed something different about the way the song sounded, all the way through. Perhaps that difference's unnameability—even the Beatles themselves might have had trouble identifying it—kept you listening to it over and over, like an itch you couldn't scratch often enough.

On the evening of February 19, 1963, the Beatles were playing one of their increasingly rare Cavern gigs—they played dozens in 1962 against a mere 11 in '63—when a telegram arrived from the *New Musical Express.* "Please Please Me," it said, had just reached No. 1. Bob Wooler announced the news, but instead of bursting into cheers, the crowd fell silent. "Everyone was stunned," recalled a Cavern regular. "That was the end of it as far as we were concerned."

The episode recalls another event, which may or may not have taken place (depending on whom you talk to) thousands of miles from Liverpool geographically and even further culturally. When the great blues singer/guitarist Robert Johnson was just a boy and not a very good musician, he disappeared for a year, to reappear as a master. Two older bluesmen, Son House and Willie Brown, were astonished. "That's little Robert? He's so good! Well, ain't that fast! He's gone now!"

The Beatles were about to make their first appearance at the Royal Albert Hall on April 18 as part of a crowded variety-show bill. Standing bored and idly backstage, Paul spotted a lovely girl with dazzling red hair and ivory skin. Never one to hold back when it was a matter of a beautiful woman, Paul walked over and chatted her up with that charm, which this woman's brother would later speak of. The other Beatles, equally smitten, all surrounded her, tossing off one-liners. After the show, everyone repaired to a friend's nearby apartment. The chatter quickly turned intimate. "They couldn't believe I was a virgin," Jane Asher said later. Lennon, always

Innocent enough: On May 19, 1967, at the press launch for the new Beatles album *Sgt. Pepper's Lonely Hearts Club Band,* a release party held at Brian Epstein's house at 24 Chapel Street in London, American photographer Linda Eastman takes pictures of Paul, whom she had met only four days earlier at the Bag O'Nails club. To be continued.

prepared to offend, asked Jane how she masturbated. "Go on, love. Tell us how girls play with themselves. We know what we do, tell us what you do." According to biographer Howard Sounes, "other crude and embarrassing sexual remarks" followed, until Paul was able to spirit Asher away. Asking for a date, he was accepted. As he said, ungallantly and even crassly, decades later, "I tried pulling her, succeeded, and we were boyfriend and girlfriend for quite a long time."

Jane Asher was only 17, four years younger than Paul, whose celebrity hers rivaled at the time. She was already a veteran actress, having appeared onstage and in movies since she was five (in a few years she would appear in the 1966 classic *Alfie* with Michael Caine). She was from an impressive family who occupied a six-floor, 18th-century town house on Wimpole Street, just across the street from the poet Elizabeth Barrett Browning's former home. Jane's father was a distinguished psychiatrist and medical researcher. He was a serious depressive and ultimately committed suicide. Mrs. Asher was a professional musician who, remarkably, had taught George Martin at Guildhall. Peter, Jane's older brother, whom we've briefly met, shortly formed that two-act, Peter and Gordon, whose Lennon-and-McCartney-penned "World Without Love" went to No. 1 in March of 1964. (Relocating later to Los Angeles, Peter would become one of the top rock producers of the '70s, working with everyone from James Taylor to Linda Ronstadt to Bonnie Raitt.)

"Paul fell like a ton of bricks for Jane," said Cynthia Lennon. "He was obviously as proud as a peacock with his new lady. For Paul, Jane Asher was a great prize." This was going to be a relationship that lasted, Paul declared to everyone within earshot. "I've always been someone who gets into a steady relationship," he said decades later. Which has never stopped him from a lifetime of slipping out the back door. Which is what eventually ended his love affair with Jane.

This photograph, taken on the tarmac in Athens, Greece, on July 22, 1967, is a study in strained emotions. Jane Asher is the woman by Paul's side, but not for much longer. Julian Lennon is the boy holding Paul's hand. Julian's dad, John, always an inattentive father to his first son, trails the pack. Julian will be the subject of Paul's song "Hey Jude." To be continued.

Paul couldn't walk the streets without being harassed by Beatlemaniacs and celebrity hounds, a state of affairs that threatened to ruin what had become a favorite activity, walking around London with Jane, who had begun taking him to hear classical music and to art galleries and museums. Hotels were fishbowls as well. Jane suggested to her mother that Paul become a houseguest of indeterminate duration, and Margaret Asher generously consented. In the autumn of 1963, Paul moved into an upstairs garret (Jane's bedroom was a decorous one floor below), shortly bringing in his piano, his record collection and other basics of life. Peter Asher's room was across the hall from Paul's, and the two bonded. Paul stayed at the Ashers' for three years, greatly enjoying the company and the food—both mother and daughter were first-rate cooks. Here was a rich and famous man, idolized by millions, living like a teenager. Perhaps this was one of many instances of Paul obsessively trying to replace his mother; we can only speculate. In any event, Margaret Asher was an extremely congenial hostess and, Paul must have fantasized, a mother. Well, mother-in-law. For it wasn't a surprise when, a few years in the future, Jane and Paul became engaged.

Paul's cultural horizon was significantly widened by the Ashers, especially around the dinner table. "It was really like culture shock in the way they ran their lives," he said later. "They would do things that I'd never seen before, like at dinner there would be word games. Now, I'm bright enough, but mine is an intuitive brightness. I could just about keep up and I could always say, 'I don't know that word.' I was always honest. In fact, I was able to enjoy and take part fully in their thing."

Did he have more complex intentions? Was he, perhaps, using the Ashers to social-climb—the uphill striving that, it seems, was part of Paul McCartney's DNA? According to the longtime Beatles public relations man Tony Barrow, Jane was "not just the girlfriend, but somebody who could lift him up that social ladder. He felt that she would be helpful to him and useful to him in progressing his march up through London society." Which, as unsympathetic a desire as this seems, is not hard to understand. A working-class kid from a crumbling town out in the provinces (as George Martin said: "The thought of anything coming out of the provinces was extraordinary at that time") was almost destined to feel second class. If John Lennon was free of social-climbing tendencies, it may have been because, alone among the Beatles, he was middle class and so probably did not feel a compulsion to rise socially. To look down on Paul for his dreams of joining the elite is itself a form of snobbery. Since he kept his middle-class aspirations under control, since he didn't harm anyone in his efforts to move up, a thoughtful observer feels more sympathy than scorn.

At least one pop masterpiece took shape in Paul's garret. He woke up one morning with an alluring melody in his head. Leaping out of bed and running to the piano, he found the right chords, and played the song over and over until it was safely lodged in his memory. But it had arrived without lyrics, and Paul couldn't come up with any. He tried for a year, testing lyrics on friends until they were sick of listening. And one day, an entire, promising verse appeared. The first word was "Yesterday."

"I wrote quite a lot of stuff up in that room, actually," said Paul later. "'I'm Looking Through You' I seem to remember coming up with after an argument with Jane." The upstairs bedroom was cramped, so when John came over for a writing session, he and Paul moved to Margaret Asher's music room in the basement. If the top floor gave birth to "Yesterday," the basement deserves its own plaque. "We wrote a lot of stuff together," John recalled, "one on one, eyeball to eyeball. Like in 'I Want to Hold Your Hand,' I remember when we got the chord that made the song. We were in Jane Asher's house, downstairs in the cellar, playing on the piano at the same time. We had 'Oh you-u-u . . . got that something . . .' and Paul hits this chord and I turn to him and say, 'That's it!' I said, 'Do it again.' In those days, we really used to absolutely write like that." This, Paul always said, was back when he and John were best friends. Yet, is there evidence that

they were more than songwriting friends? The two always had very different outlooks and personalities. A rebel since his teens, John loathed the showbiz polish that Brian Epstein had imposed on the Beatles, while Paul, the opportunistic careerist, loved it. Were they, in fact, as close as we sense they were? It's so complicated.

In 1963, just a few months after the release of "Love Me Do," the Beatles put out four singles: "Please Please Me" (released on January 11), "From Me to You" (April 11), "She Loves You" (August 23) and "I Want to Hold Your Hand" (November 29). Even as cocky as they were, they never expected the records to do as spectacularly well as they did. All four flew to the top of the singles charts (unless you want to quibble about "Please Please Me").

"She Loves You" exceeded everyone's—*everyone's*—expectations. Entering the charts on August 31, it stayed there for 31 weeks. It reached No. 1 on September 14, stayed there for a month, dropped off and came back on November 30.

After listening a few times to "She Loves You," you realize that it's the cliché itself—a breath of fresh air, a counterstatement to the same old two-guys-fighting-over-the-girl formula. Tossing out that shibboleth, Lennon and McCartney have Guy No. 1 ("You think you've lost your love . . .") sympathetically urging Guy No. 2 back to the girl he jilted ("She says you hurt her so / She almost lost her mind . . ."). And Guy No. 1 gives his final, strongest piece of advice: "Pride can hurt you too / Apologize to her . . ." Not too many people in 1963, and then in America in 1964, heard the message. What got all the attention (not surprisingly) were those two little ornaments, now called hooks: "Yeah, yeah, yeah!" and that Little Richard rip-off "Ooooh!"

Two albums appeared in 1963, *Please Please Me* (released on March 22) and *With the Beatles* (on that awful day stateside, November 22). The former hit the top of the British charts in May, remaining there for 30 weeks before being displaced by *With the Beatles*, which occupied the top of the charts for 21 weeks. In other words, the Beatles owned the top spot for 51 consecutive weeks. Only the soundtrack to *South Pacific*, which lodged at No. 1 on the British charts from fall 1958 to spring 1960, stayed at the top of the British charts longer than *Please Please Me*.

Why did the Beatles' 1963 records, singles and albums both, sell so spectacularly well, so early on in their recording career, when they were still unknowns?

The answer is that they weren't in the least unknown, thanks to Brian Epstein's canny—especially for a neophyte manager—strategy of putting the band on what has elsewhere been called "The Never-Ending Tour." Epstein booked the boys into what seemed to them to be every dump in Britain and then sent them back, seeding the provinces with future Beatles record buyers. In 1962, the Beatles played an unbelievable 354 shows, often two a day. If this was exhausting for the band, it paid off big-time, with the massive sales of the single "Please Please Me," the album of the same name and the Beatles' other record-setting 1963 releases.

Don't knock marketing, even of the primitive and rubber-burning sort. Let's travel six thousand miles to Los Angeles, where, in the first week of December 1963, a group of executives at Capitol Records, the Beatles' American label, are shaken out of their torpor to see in the new *Variety* how these Beatles' "She Loves You" and "I Want to Hold Your Hand" have each sold a million copies, the most ever except for Elvis's 1957 double-sided hit "Hound Dog/Don't Be Cruel." "Thus in a matter of days was Capitol consumed by a spirit of . . . Beatlemania," writes Gould.

Here are a small percentage of the publicity moves taken at the end of 1963 and the beginning of 1964 by Capitol and other music- and entertainment-business players: Capitol asked Brian Epstein for a new Beatles album to coincide with the group's first, February 9 appearance on *The Ed Sullivan Show*. Capitol also planned to release half a million stickers reading, "The Beatles Are Coming!" à la Paul Revere along with a mock newspaper with the front-page headline "Beatlemania Sweeps U.S.!" and to outfit the entire Capitol sales staff with Beatle wigs. Prime-time television news got involved—on December 10, the *CBS Evening News* aired a clip of the Beatles

Even before the Beatles formally disband, they informally disband. Paul was the only musician featured on the song discussed on the previous pages, "Martha My Dear," and many other cuts on the double-disc set *The Beatles* (a.k.a. the *White Album*) are executed by only one or two members of the quartet. On some tracks where folks did try to contribute, Paul might have criticized the playing. Ringo will later say how wonderful it was to record "Yer Blues" because it was all four of them again, with a downbeat, like in the old days. It should be said: That spirit would briefly be rekindled, thanks to the urgings of George Martin and Paul, with the recording of *Abbey Road*—but we are now in the period when the four who were once so interdependent are, almost suddenly, at swords' points. Paul is in an interesting place: so ready to show and get independent credit for his work, and so in love with the idea of his band. After John makes his internal declaration in September 1969 that he is leaving the Beatles, Paul goes home and starts taping the material that will become, in April 1970, his first solo album, *McCartney*.

For just a second, when you contemplate this 1969 Linda McCartney portrait, think back to the beginning of the decade, to where these two were. Back then, they were in leathers, in Hamburg or Liverpool, their hair greased, sweating bullets and smiling ear to ear (probably high as kites) as they worked their way through set after set of mostly other people's rock 'n' roll or rhythm and blues. If their eyes were set to the future, the future was only tomorrow, and beyond that was something far more amorphous: the dream. In the intervening years, the dream was realized in incomprehensible ways. Now, in 1969, they know that they have made one last great album, *Abbey Road,* and on this day—August 8—they are assembled to pose for Iain Macmillan's camera at a crosswalk on Abbey Road in north London, just outside the recording studio. Paul has sketched the game plan in pencil. He wants to show the four of them walking away from what they have made there in the past seven years. A bobby holds up traffic while Macmillan makes six photographs on this uncommonly hot day. During downtime, Linda takes informal pictures, and in this one John and Paul talk things over. Nothing is as it was in the old days. But in aspects (tension, guessing, competition, need, affection), it is weirdly like the old days. Paul, now running the band, chooses Macmillan's fifth frame as the cover. One more—one last—brilliant decision in the Beatles years.

performing in Britain before a crowd of hysterical girls—and so did radio, sponsoring Beatles-related contests, playing bootlegged Beatles interviews and, after it was officially released, playing "I Want to Hold Your Hand" as often as the weather report.

Released in the U.S. on December 26, "I Want to Hold Your Hand" entered the American charts three weeks later. A mere two weeks after that, it hit No. 1, having sold a million copies. In New York City, 10 thousand records were being sold per hour.

The greatness of the Beatles' music certainly played the largest part in the group's almost instant rise to American popularity. But in trying to comprehend the miraculous-seeming swiftness of the group's ascent, one can't discount the advance work—in Britain, by Brian Epstein and the Beatles themselves; in the U.S., by corporate-backed publicity—that played an indispensable role in the band's astounding success. But regardless, there was the joy and the moment. On January 16, the Beatles were playing the Olympia theater in Paris. "One night," recalled Paul, "we arrived back at the hotel from the Olympia, when a telegram came through to Brian from Capitol Records of America. He came running into the room saying, 'Hey, look! You are No. 1 in America!'"

You'll see that instant, later in our pages, in one of the famous "pillow fight" photos shot by then–Fleet Streeter and subsequently longtime LIFE contributor Harry Benson. It was the moment that solidified the change. Everything had, however, already changed: Their destiny was their own. Everything had already sped up and was about to speed up further.

Harry Benson remembered recently at his apartment in Manhattan, "Paul made sure to have the pillow. He made sure to be in charge of the action."

As we have already seen—Paul was becoming more himself; they were all becoming more themselves. Almost as soon as it finally came together, which took seven years, it would start coming apart, which would take barely four.

As Paul would be lucky enough to realize in his life: It was all but impossible to be a Beatle, but he could be himself.

P an Am Flight 101 rocketed east to west across the Atlantic on February 7, 1964—50 years ago—bearing four rather insecure but lovable mop-tops. Paul was hardly envisioning any British Invasion and, echoing George's anxiety, asked a rhetorical question: "They've got their own groups. What are we going to give them that they don't already have?" At Kennedy airport, 3,000 excited Beatlemaniacs were waiting to greet them. When the lads first glimpsed the crowd, they figured the President must be landing. As they exited their plane, it became readily apparent that the screams were for them—and that the shrieks for Paul dwarfed those for his mates.

Two days after their arrival, the Beatles furthered their conquest of America in spectacular fashion. In the first of four live appearances on *The Ed Sullivan Show,* they drew an audience of more than 73 million, over a third of America's 1964 population and a record for U.S. television. The critics clearly didn't know what to make of these four young men, but they pretended they did. John S. Wilson of *The New York Times:* "[The Beatles] are merely taking advantage of that sound old laissez faire theory that there's a sucker born every minute." LIFE magazine, as much an American arbiter at the time as any nationwide mainstream media outlet, all but ignored the phenomenon—for the moment. Others, a little more "out there" or "with it," had already been sucked in, sensing something happening. "I remember hearing 'I Want to Hold Your Hand,' and all of a sudden, for the first time in my life, I started dancing," remembered the poet Allen Ginsberg. "It seemed that the years of wartime repression were really over, or something was over, and the new era had begun. People were returning back into their bodies unafraid and were celebrating their physical existence—the dance, which is an old, human ritual. Everybody was moved to dance."

That's not a bad description of one kind of human behavior that would be unleashed in the 1960s, certainly with the Beatles' help, but consider what it looked like from inside the frenzy, from the eye of the storm. It looked scary.

Glanced at in retrospect, the Beatles story becomes clear: The beginning of it all really was, in this case, the beginning of the end of it all. Everything would become surreal from this point for the band, and even as the Beatles would rise musically, the Beatles would descend personally. George will be fed up with—and terrified by—live performance by the end of the first U.S. concert, in Washington, D.C., two days after the historic appearance on the *Sullivan* show.

The nuttiness of the Washington gig would be replicated time and again in the next several months. Although *The Washington Post* had described the Beatles as "asexual and homely," more than 7,000 fans jammed the Coliseum to decide for themselves. At a British Embassy reception, as the group obligingly signed autographs, one upper-class twit asked, "Can they actually write?" Another walked up to Ringo and cut off a piece of his hair. When British prime minister Sir Alec Douglas-Home arrived at the White House the day after the concert for a meeting with President Lyndon Johnson, LBJ was all smiles. "I like your advance guard," he said. "But don't you think they need haircuts?" The boundaries of the generation gap had been demarcated, and the Beatles were promoted as generals of their side in the coming fray.

There would be other colonels, majors and lieutenants, some of whom would influence the Beatles' direction. On August 28, 1964, Bob Dylan appeared at the posh Delmonico Hotel in Manhattan to meet them. After some small talk, Dylan decided to turn the boys on. None of the Beatles had smoked marijuana. John, still too apprehensive to give it a try, "hands [the joint] to Ringo," writes Dylan's friend and courtier Al Aronowitz, "making a remark about Ringo being his royal taste tester. That shows you the Beatles' pecking order. Paul got high and seemed to think it was the first time he had ever done some real thinking, so he had [the Beatles' man Friday] Mal Evans follow him around with a pad and pencil and write down everything he said." A direct offshoot of Dylan's visit: Paul became a devoted pothead who would be repeatedly arrested for possession.

How deep would be the divide between the "kids" and the "establishment"? After the Beatles were made Members of the Order of the British Empire on June 11, 1965, at a Buckingham Palace ceremony (John: "I thought you had to drive tanks and win wars to get the MBE"), "a dozen of the queen's most distinguished subjects sent back their own medals," in the words of author Nicholas Schaffner. "A Canadian politician said he no longer wanted his because it put him 'on the same level with vulgar nincompoops.'"

The remaining Beatles years were simply a march of strength on strength, accompanied by a downward spiral of discomfort, abject fear (if not quite paranoia), escalating drug use, recrimination, breakups and mendings, and finally a sundering that stuck. It seemed to the others that Paul was seeking control of the band, and, worn out by the tension and constant bickering, John ceded it. Here we highlight the triumphant and tumultuous and eventually sad tale:

- **August 6, 1965** "Yesterday" is released. The McCartney composition, recorded solo by Paul, backed by a string quartet playing a George Martin arrangement, is the first Beatles song by just one group member. "Yesterday" has been covered by more artists—upwards of 2,200—than any other song in recording history. It is currently ranked 13th on *Rolling Stone's* "Top 500 Greatest Songs of All Time."

- **August 15, 1965** In the first appearance of a musical act at a sports stadium, the Beatles pack Shea Stadium, home of the New York Mets. The capacity crowd of 55,600, the majority of whom are the usual screaming girls, howls to beat the band, as it were. "[The fans'] immature lungs," writes *Times*man Murray Schumach, "produced a sound so staggering, so massive, so shrill and sustained, that it quickly crossed the line from enthusiasm into hysteria and was soon in the area of the classic Greek meaning of the word *pandemonium*, the region of all demons."

On January 30, 1969, the Beatles take to the rooftop at Apple Corps in London for what will be their final live performance, and although the chronology is slightly off—as was the order of release of their last two albums—we run this photo just *after* the one of John and Paul sitting on Abbey Road, since Paul's gesture here seems to be saying: "That's it, enough, goodbye." *Let It Be* was a painful mess to make, if indeed it can be said that the Beatles made it. (They certainly did not, not in the kind of uniform, ordered way they made their albums with George Martin.) The film version of the process puts the interband acrimony on full display, and if Paul thought it was boldly confessional and *honest* back in the day, he has since been party to Beatles efforts to suppress it because it does nothing but tarnish the Fab Four's—and particularly his—legacy. The rooftop concert, in the cold, was pretty good and made everyone wonder what might have been. Consider: If John and Paul had, pre-*Abbey Road*, been more welcoming of George's progress, and if they had still been at least listening to and influencing each other's songs, what might the next three or four Beatles albums have been, with the material on *All Things Must Pass, McCartney, Ram, Plastic Ono Band* and *Imagine* thrown into the magical blender that was the Beatles? Goodness!

He's on his own—he's McCartney now, not Paul. In the years and decades that follow, that equation will go back and forth, and he will wrestle with its implications or embrace his Paulhood, depending on his situation and relative feelings of security. But in 1970, the Beatles are history, and he (each of them, actually) is getting a major "slagging" for that bald fact. In the public's opinion: "It's his fault." "It's John's fault." "It's Yoko's fault." "It's Linda's fault." "His solo album stinks." "John's solo album stinks." "John's is great; his is great." (Everyone feels George's is great, as well it might be, since it's packed with fine songs he'd written in the past few years that couldn't, or wouldn't, be squeezed on to the Lennon/McCartney-dominated Beatles albums.) "I remember Ringo saying at the time," Paul recalled in 1974 to Paul Gambaccini of *Rolling Stone*, "'How many friends have I got?' And he couldn't count them on one hand. And that's what it boils down to, really. You can have millions of friends, but when someone asks you how many friends you've got, it depends on how honestly you're going to answer. Because I don't think I've got that many. No one went against me or anything, I think I isolated myself a bit. It's just one of those things."

- **"After the show,"** continues Schumach, "a girl knelt on the field, sobbing, 'Please, please, give us some blades of grass. They walked on the grass.' A passing policewoman observed, 'They are psychos. Their mothers ought to see them now.'"

- **For the band,** the evening is, as the expression goes, a good job of work. A half hour onstage gets the boys $160,000, or $1.2 million in today's dollars.

- **December 6, 1965** *Rubber Soul* is released. "The time had come to experiment," says the Beatles' producer, George Martin, later. "The Beatles knew it, and I knew it." *Rubber Soul* marks the start of the far-ranging musical explorations that will occupy the Beatles for the balance of their partnership. "*Rubber Soul* broke everything open," says the rock 'n' roll great Steve Winwood. "It crossed music into a whole new dimension and was responsible for kicking off the '60s rock era as we know it."

- **August 8, 1966** *Revolver* is released. More adventurous still than *Rubber Soul*, *Revolver* is the band's first sustained effort to loosen, if not discard, the day's musical and lyrical conventions. The album has a greater yield of classics than any preceding Beatles disc: "Taxman" (screaming lead guitar by Paul); the impossible-to-dislike "Yellow Submarine," sung by the impossible-to-dislike Ringo; and, with a little writing help from John, Paul's haunting "Eleanor Rigby." (Jerry Leiber, a master songwriter from an earlier era, says, "I don't think there's ever been a better song written.") As a contrast, closing the album is John's "Tomorrow Never Knows," *Revolver*'s farthest-out song by a long shot. There is no longer any question of who's behind what, vis-à-vis Paul and John.

- **August 29, 1966** It's a closely guarded secret: The concert tonight at San Francisco's Candlestick Park will be the Beatles' last; they're bidding a not-fond farewell to the highway. Pressure to stop touring will not have emanated from Paul's corner—he's the band's road warrior. But George has said "No more," and John has agreed. "I always remember to thank Jesus for the end of my touring days," John later says. "If I hadn't said that the Beatles were 'bigger than Jesus' and upset the very Christian Ku Klux Klan, well, Lord, I might still be up there with all the other performing fleas! God bless America. Thank you, Jesus."

- **May 15, 1967** Paul meets Linda Eastman, a young American photographer of rock stars, at a London club. A product of well-to-do Scarsdale, New York, Linda dates, as well as works, in the rock scene. Long before she meets him, she announces to a friend that she will marry Paul McCartney.

- **June 2, 1967** *Sgt. Pepper's Lonely Hearts Club Band* is released. If any album is rock's greatest, it's this, the Beatles' eighth. But despite its brilliance, *Sgt. Pepper* contains a major flaw. According to Paul, he wanted to make an album played entirely by a fictitious band. In other words, the record was going to be a rock opera, with an entire cast of characters, two years before the Who's *Tommy*. But for some reason, Paul lets his imaginary world die after only two songs, the title track and "With a Little Help from My Friends," starring Ringo as "Billy Shears." And then we go directly into "Lucy in the Sky with Diamonds," totally unrelated to the vanished narrative of the good sergeant. Formwise, the rest of *Sgt. Pepper* is just another conventional album, i.e., a sequence of unrelated songs. Somehow, Paul seems to think his concept has held up. Yet despite the greatness of "A Day in the Life" and all the rest, *Sgt. Pepper*'s underlying concept, as conceived by Paul, peters out almost before it begins.

- **August 27, 1967** Brian Epstein dies. The Beatles' indispensable manager is in his London town house when he succumbs to an overdose of sleeping pills. Although Epstein had multiple drug addictions, his death is ruled accidental. It's worth quoting Paul's assessment a second time: "If

anyone was the Fifth Beatle, it was Brian." John doesn't disagree. As he says later, "After Brian died, we collapsed. The Beatles broke up after Brian died."

- **July 20, 1968** In an appearance on the BBC-TV chat show *Dee Time*, Jane Asher announces the end of her five-year romance with Paul, this despite their engagement on the previous Christmas Day. Asher has two main reasons for initiating the breakup: first, Paul's pestering of his fiancée to throw over a healthy acting career for housewifery (Asher confides in Cynthia Lennon, John's ex, "that Paul wanted me to become the little woman at home with the kiddies") and, second, his compulsive infidelity. An instance of the latter is the immediate cause of the separation. Jane appears at Paul's house to find him in bed with a casual, part-time girlfriend. Jane exits on the spot, furious of course. Almost immediately, her mother appears at Paul's, gathers her daughter's belongings without a word to Jane's soon-to-be-ex-fiancé and lets herself out. Jane has taken permanent leave of a lover who has consistently undervalued her.

- **August 22, 1968** Ringo exits. During the recording of the *White Album*, Paul criticizes Ringo's playing on Paul's song "Back in the USSR." Ringo leaves in a huff, goes home to pack and heads to Sardinia for a week of sulking. A telegram arrives, saying, "You're the best rock and roll drummer in the world. Come on home, we love you." Somewhat mollified, Ringo packs up and comes home. "Paul," Ringo says later, "is the greatest bass player in the world. But he is also very determined to get his own way."

- **March 12, 1969** Paul and Linda wed at Marylebone Register Office in London—it's his first marriage, her second; she's 27, he's 26; she's got a six-year-old daughter from her first marriage, whom Paul will adopt. Paul has bought a £12 ring for Linda the evening before the wedding, "just before the shop shut," he remembers much later. "We had a big argument that night and it was nearly called off. We were very up and down, quite funky compared to the image of '25 years of married bliss!' . . . You get this picture of us swanning along in a little rowboat, managing to avoid the white water, but we were right in the middle of that white water, man, so it's miraculous that we made it. But we did." No other Beatles are at the wedding. "I really don't remember whether or not I invited any of the band," Paul says in *The Beatles Anthology*. "I'm a total bastard, I suppose."

- **September 20, 1969** At a summit meeting of all four Beatles, John announces, "I want a divorce." Paul, who has rightly been called "the beatlest Beatle," takes his band's impending collapse the hardest, suffering what he later calls "a breakdown." "It was a pretty good job to have lost—the Beatles," he says. "I took to my bed, didn't bother shaving much, did a lot of drinking . . . I lost the plot there for a little while." John and George are at loose ends, too, in the immediate aftermath. The only clearheaded Beatle is Ringo, keeping away from the madness, working contentedly on his first solo album, *Sentimental Journey*. "If [Lennon's demand] had happened in 1965, or 1967 even," says the drummer, "it would have been a mighty shock. Now it was just 'Let's get the divorce over with.'"

- **October 1, 1969** *Abbey Road* is released. Although it's the last Beatles album recorded, *Abbey Road* is released before the previously recorded *Let It Be*. The gem of side one is George's classic "Something" (which one of its many interpreters called "the greatest love song ever written"—that's Ol' Blue Eyes speaking). Side two is everybody's favorite half of a Beatles album, with producer George Martin stitching eight songs into a seamless medley. Every song no doubt has its 5 million adherents, but our favorite is not even a song, just a tiny part of one. Three words. Namely, Paul's sublimely screamed "smiles awake you" in "Golden Slumbers." These few seconds are not merely Paul's best singing on *Abbey Road*, but in the *entire* Beatles oeuvre. That's one opinion, anyway. But go back and relisten.

On the opposite page: The civil wedding of Paul McCartney and Linda Eastman at Marylebone Register Office in London on March 12, 1969, with Linda's six-year-old daughter, Heather, from her previous marriage to American geologist Joseph Melville See Jr., in attendance. Thus begins perhaps the greatest and most acclaimed (justly acclaimed!) marriage in rock 'n' roll history. Keith Richards and Patti Hansen's is pretty good, and Bruce and Patty. But Paul and Linda? The gold standard. At the outset, everyone hated her, not least because Paul put her in the band. He told *Rolling Stone* he didn't care about the reaction, but he could have handled it differently: "If you write millions of love songs . . . finally when you're in love you'd kind of like to write one for the person you're in love with. So I think all this business about getting Linda in the billing was just a way of saying, 'Listen, I don't care what you think, this is what I think. I'm putting her right up there with me.' Later we thought it might have been cooler not to introduce her so bluntly. Perhaps a little more show business: 'Ladies and gentlemen, I'd like to introduce you to my better half. Isn't she sweet and coy?'"

Paul and Linda walking near their East Sussex home in Peasmarsh, of which we will learn more in the caption on the pages immediately following. Paul, after a decade of high intensity, seeks a country idyll. He and Linda build one.

Above are Paul and Linda with newborn daughter Stella on September 17, 1971. At right: They have, in the summer of 1974, transported their down-home act to Nashville, where they are rehearsing with the band. Paul's was an interesting duality: He was (and wanted to be, and still wants to be) one of the greatest rockers ever, a basher, a screamer. But he wanted (and still wants) his measure of peace and relative quiet. He tried to construct the latter in rural Peasmarsh near Rye in East Sussex. He bought a 160-acre plot there in the 1970s, and he and Linda lived in the cottage on what was called Blossom Wood Farm until it became evident that their growing family would require a better, or at least a somewhat bigger, house. Paul took control, planning the replacement, which would be larger but still modest. Said David Litchfield, a friend and Linda's former employer at *Ritz* magazine: "While Paul was rich enough to hire a world-class architect and spare no expense in creating the ultimate in rural luxury, it wasn't his, or Linda's, style. Instead he sat down at the kitchen table and designed the family home himself—a rather plain redbrick house with no extravagant features." Here they would raise their family, in what a friend described as "a glorified council house." Much later, Heather McCartney, Paul's second wife, would detest the property in Peasmarsh, and it would be cited more than once in her divorce complaint.

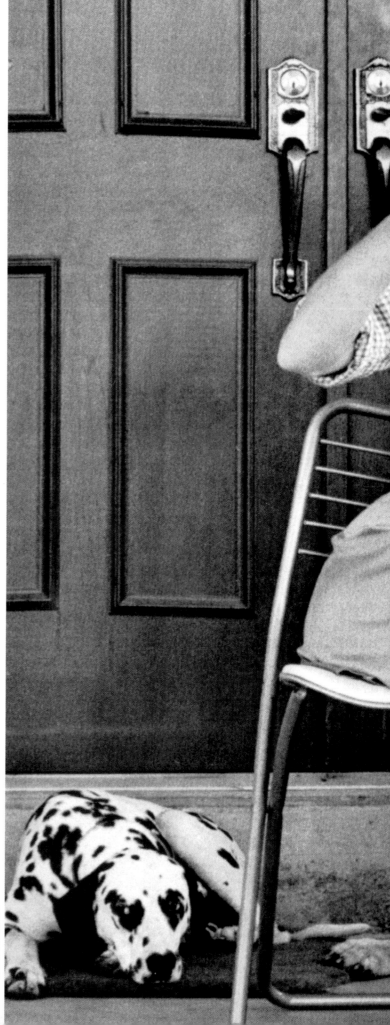

- **April 20, 1970** Paul's first solo album, *McCartney,* is released with a press kit lambasting the other Beatles. On the one hand, *McCartney* demonstrates Paul's versatility— he plays every instrument and sings all parts, except for a few harmonies by Linda. Yet almost everything on *McCartney* is pap. The sole exception is "Maybe I'm Amazed," perhaps the best song of Paul's solo career. With all of the rest, one wonders, "Does the guy think that every crappy song he tosses off is a masterpiece because it's *his*?" Already a murmur arises, later a cry: *"He needs John!"*

- **May 18, 1970** *Let It Be* is released, the final Beatles album to hit the racks. It's hardly the Beatles' best; still, it has one or two songs for the ages: Paul's quasi-prayer of a title song, a genuine classic, and "The Long and Winding Road," a lovely McCartney ballad almost ruined by guest producer Phil Spector's sappy strings. But overall, *Let It Be* is not a very strong last testament. The Beatles should indeed have switched its release with that of *Abbey Road.* The latter would not only have made a much more memorable closing statement, it has the most appropriate possible final song: "The End."

- **December 31, 1970** Paul files suit against the other three to dissolve the 1967 contract that binds the Beatles' finances together. The group is not legally sundered until 1975, by which time all four former Beatles have solo careers and are speaking to one another only intermittently.

That wouldn't be the end of it, of course (and we're not just talking about legacy or future sales or "found" releases here). John fired an early post-Beatles salvo in a 1971, two-part interview in *Rolling Stone.* He says that Paul's first solo album was "rubbish"; that the film *Let It Be* was "set up by Paul for Paul. That is one of the main reasons the Beatles ended. I can't speak for George, but I pretty damn well know we got fed up of being sidemen for Paul"; that Paul's reaction to Lennon's first solo LP will be that it will "scare him into doing

something decent"; et cetera. Paul stayed mum at the time and answered John by forming a new band, Wings. Throughout the 1970s, after his second solo album, *Ram,* was out of the way, Wings would be his musical vehicle.

What was Wings, and what is there to say of it? Wings was a best-selling (six No. 1 singles and four No. 1 albums in the U.S.), critically savaged, mutating musical agglomeration led by Paul, with Linda on backup vocals and keyboards, and a revolving cast of sidemen. Linda was a nonmusician; worse, she was lacking the least glimmer of musical talent, and even an alchemist such as Paul couldn't change the fact. But she would be in the band because Paul said so. "It was never Linda's desire to perform live with Paul, she did it to please him," Howard Sounes writes. To please him, yes: He wanted her near, always, to soothe and nurture him. Linda, for the full decade of Wings' existence, attracted almost nightly ridicule for her off-key vocals—some of the criticism horribly meanspirited. After Wings was good and grounded, Linda defended herself and Paul thusly: "We thought we were in it for the fun . . . it was just something we wanted to do, so if we got it wrong, big deal. We don't have to justify ourselves." Paul, too, was wholly unapologetic, usually responding to critics with yet another silly love song. "Ballads and babies," he said, "that's what's happened to me." (Linda and Paul's biological children together—Mary, Stella and James—were born between 1969 and 1977.)

Quite obviously, the McCartneys had nothing to apologize for. If the fans didn't want to buy the records or tickets to the shows, no one was making them. If other Beatles worshippers preferred John's discs, fine. His *Imagine* album is rightly considered a classic, and Paul's *Band on the Run,* released in 1973, remains an indisputably fine album; *Rolling Stone*'s demanding Jon Landau, for one, called it upon its release "a carefully composed, intricately designed personal statement, and (with the possible exception of John Lennon's *Plastic Ono Band*) the finest record yet released by any of the four musicians who were once called the Beatles." So Wings worked smoothly for the McCartneys in a decade that, in and of itself, is derided by cultural historians as superfluous. Some of the

Clockwise from top left, opposite: Three scenes from the life of Wings in 1975. First we have Paul and Linda in their dressing room in, of all places, Liverpool. Then the husband and wife are in the midst of a sound check at the Elstree rehearsal studio in London. Finally, during those rehearsals at Elstree, daughter Stella seeks refuge and sucks her thumb while Mum and Dad finish their work. (Stella McCartney will, of course, grow to become a celebrated fashion designer.) Said Paul to *Rolling Stone* at about this time: "You still end up thinking, well, it's my life. I know a lot of rock 'n' roll stars or just even show business people who will regulate their life to their image. It can mess you up a lot. I know a lot of guys from the old days who wouldn't get married, even if they wanted to. Wouldn't get married because it might affect their careers . . . But the thing is, in a couple of years, his career is over anyway. And he didn't get married, and he went and blew it. So I didn't. 'Well, I'm not going to let that kind of thing interfere with *me*.' Although I didn't wish to blow my career, I thought it was more important to get on with living. We just went ahead and just did what we felt like doing. Some of it came out possibly a bit offensive to some people, but it turns out that it didn't matter in the first place. You just keep going."

There was never really any rivalry between the Beatles and the Stones, simply because, throughout the 1960s, Lennon and McCartney—two guys who could get rivalrous with the best of them—were always a step ahead. Heck, they gave the Stones their first Top 20 hit: "I Wanna Be Your Man." And so, years later in 1978, it is all hunky-dory backstage in New York City, with Ron Wood (above) and (opposite) Bill Wyman and a sashaying Mick Jagger. Linda has had enough of it, apparently, but Paul is a glad-handing guest. Later still, he will seek respite from his troubled second marriage with afternoon chat sessions at Keith Richards's Caribbean retreat.

Wings output can in fact be seen as high points of the '70s.

And then came the 1980s, and the intrusion of life itself.

Disembarking at Tokyo's Narita International Airport for a Wings tour of Japan on January 16, 1980, Paul could only watch in horror as a customs official turned up eight ounces of marijuana in one of his suitcases. Drug possession was a serious offense in Japan, and Paul, again to his horror, faced a possible prison sentence. Handcuffed, he was taken to jail, where he slept with his back to the wall to avoid being raped. Eventually, his mood lightened. During a group shower, he led the other prisoners in a sing-along of "Yellow Submarine." After nine days, he was released, provided that he confessed and promised not to return to Japan for seven years. He did as asked and beat it out of there.

At the tail end of that year, on December 8, John Lennon was murdered in New York City. About to enter his apartment building, John was shot and killed by a psychotic fan named Mark David Chapman. Paul got the news right away. Though devastated, he decided to go to work (he would later learn that George did the same). After a day at AIR Studios, Paul left and was quickly surrounded by reporters, who would not stop grilling him. Trying to conclude the interrogation, Paul started toward his car and said, "Yeah, it's a drag, isn't it?"

The moment that the indifferent-sounding comment left his lips, Paul wished he hadn't uttered it. The news immediately went out: "Paul McCartney reacts in a crass and hard-hearted fashion."

"A 'drag' isn't how the world will see it," said a stern-faced newscaster.

Sounes tries to provide some background: "Just as when his mother and father had died," writes the biographer, "and when Stuart Sutcliffe passed away, Paul had reacted awkwardly to death, saying and doing the wrong thing." Some handle such things better than others do, and some can't handle them in public very well at all.

A footnote first, and then a postscript: In

1973, John left Yoko for a 14-month affair with their assistant May Pang (a childhood friend, incidentally, of Linda McCartney's). Paul found him on the left coast, daily drunk, and urged a reconciliation with his wife. Lennon eventually returned to New York City, and he and Yoko became a couple again and stayed together until his death. Make of that what you will, but it appears, on paper, a brotherly intervention.

The postscript: It has taken McCartney years to accept without ambivalence his love for John Lennon, and even today, in the new millennium, there is conflict. The passion of their relationship, even when their friendship was at its periods of low ebb, indicates that love was there when they were teenagers, love was at work through the period of competition and jealousy when they were two successful artists, and love was behind the angry words as well as the conciliatory gestures of the post-Beatles years.

It's there today, long after John has gone—a confused love that the two men always wrestled with, and Paul wrestles with still. "He could be a right bastard," Paul says in *The Beatles Anthology*, first published in 2000. "But all in all, deep down, and having said that, he was a great person to know. He was a very charismatic guy. I was a bit of a John fan. I think we all were. And I think we had a mutual admiration going on there."

Even for those, including Paul, who had once seen Wings as a propulsive band, that vehicle ran out of gas, and in 1981, with sidemen peeling off one by one and the leader himself having lost interest, the idea just sort of drifted away. With the opposite of the front-page shock that greeted the dissolution of the Beatles, Wings went out with a whimper, not a bang. Paul was perfectly okay with this. "I used to think that all my Wings stuff was second rate," he would tell *Playboy* magazine a few years on, before catching himself with a modest amendment: "Even I have to admit there definitely was something there with some of the Wings songs." He has continued to play some of those songs in his live act, and in 2013 would energetically promote the anniversary

reissue of the live album, *Wings over America*. Paul likes some parts of his backstory more than others, and some of his past recorded output more than the rest, but is confident that all of it has value because it is about, or done by, Paul McCartney. He once doubted Paul McCartney; he no longer does.

The young, then-hot producer Hugh Padgham found this out in spades in 1985 when he was hired by the now-solo Paul to coproduce *Press to Play*, which when it was released would be regarded well (the *Chicago Tribune*'s Lynn Van Matre: "No doubt about it, this is McCartney's most rocking album in ages. Much of it's catchy, most of it's fun, and it's superior to McCartney's efforts of recent years") but today is seen as second- or third-tier. McCartney emerged from the Beatles and now the Wings years as a self-perceived elder statesman, sure of himself, and it would take added maturity to sandpaper this conceit to any kind of smoothness. "All the people who work for him," Padgham grumbled after the project had been concluded, "if he said jump, they'd go, 'From what floor?' . . . If you think that McCartney probably hasn't been able to walk down the street without somebody wanting to kiss his arse from the age of 17 . . . I imagine it would affect you, possibly in an insidious way . . . If he doesn't get his own way, then he throws his toys out of the pram." Listening to a song in progress, Padgham had the chutzpah to tell the boss, "I don't think it's good enough."

"Hugh," Paul shot back, "when did you write your last No. 1?"

"That one was a real kick in the balls," Padgham said, "which you don't forget." Padgham, writes Sounes, "lived an increasingly miserable existence, as work on this difficult album dragged on for an amazing 18 months, the producer becoming thoroughly fed up with Paul McCartney in the process."

If John Lennon could be a right bastard, as his friends and enemies admitted, the über-controlling Paul McCartney, too, had his moments. Especially after the death of John, whose presence near or far had always engendered insecurity and restraint in Paul, the truly solo artist became super-confident and bold.

Paul is seen here on the Upper West Side of Manhattan in 1982. The cognoscenti among you are immediately twigging to the fact that this is near where John Lennon was killed two years earlier. Yes, it is. But Paul is running away from nothing. He is starting to embrace it all. (In this decade, he will finally start singing some of his Beatles songs again in live performance, overcoming the thumb-in-your-eye petulance that plagued him during the Wings years.) He releases in '82 his first solo album since Wings was dissolved and John was killed, *Tug of War*. It is produced by George Martin, with whom he was working when he awoke to learn John had been shot. He and Martin had reconvened, dabbled and then felt it best to walk away, take a break and deal with their grief. They got back together, though, working with Stevie Wonder and Carl Perkins among several others. "Ebony and Ivory" went to No. 1 all over the world, as did *Tug of War* in many countries. Everyone wanted Paul back, and he granted everyone their wish. He was back.

HOMER SYKES/CAMERA PRESS/REDUX

20TH CENTURY FOX/EVERETT

But even boldness at its furthest reach can be, like McCartney himself, endearing. Though he still can neither read nor write music ("I prefer to think of myself as a primitive," McCartney has said, "rather like the primitive cave artists who drew without training"), Paul, in 1991, tried his hand at orchestral music. "For years, I have been flirting with classical music," he said. "On 'Yesterday' I had a string quartet and on 'Eleanor Rigby' we had used string players, so I always enjoyed the experience. And in the back of my mind, there was always this thought that if I ever get a great offer to do something big in the classical world, I'd leap at it." Reviews for his heartfelt *Liverpool Oratorio* were mixed—"honest" said one critic and "inspiring" declared another; *The New York Times* said, "There are moments of beauty and pleasure in this dramatic miscellany . . . the music's innocent sincerity makes it difficult to be put off by its ambitions," while London's *Guardian* griped that there is "little awareness of the need for recurrent ideas that will bind the work into a whole"—but all of that is ultimately inconsequential, as Paul, soon to be Sir Paul, is off to the next thing. Maybe it will be an album of rock songs sung live in Moscow or on MTV, or new introspective material, or an art show. Who knows, who cares? He is Paul McCartney. The joke about how he "used to be in a band before Wings" becomes an old and tired joke, as it deserves to be perceived. He's Paul McCartney.

On January 19, 1994, Paul is a speaker at John Lennon's induction as a solo artist into the Rock and Roll Hall of Fame. Speaking as if to his old friend, Paul recalls episodes from their shared past: "I remember introducing you to my mate George, my schoolmate, and him getting into the group by playing 'Raunchy' on the top deck of the bus. You were impressed. And we met Ringo, who'd been working the whole season at Butlin's holiday camp. He was a seasoned professional, but the beard had to go, and it did.

"We'd been on a van touring and we'd have the kind of night where the windscreen would break. We'd be on the motorway going back up to Liverpool. It was freezing, so we had to lie on top of each other in the back of the van, creating a Beatle sandwich. These were the ways we got to know each other.

"We got to Hamburg and met the likes of Little Richard. I remember Little Richard inviting us back to his hotel. He was looking at Ringo's ring. He said, 'I love that ring.' He said, 'I've got a ring like that. I could give you a ring like that.' So we all went back to the hotel with him. We never got a ring.

"We went back with Gene Vincent to his hotel once. It was all going fine, until he reached into his bedside drawer and he pulled out a gun. We said, 'Well, we've got to go, Gene. We've got to go.' And we got out quick!

"So now, years on, here we are. All these people. Here we are, assembled, to thank you for everything you mean to all of us.

"This letter comes with love, from your friend Paul."

Linda died at 56 from breast cancer in 1998 during a family getaway in Tanque Verde, Arizona. Paul told the *Daily Mail* that after his wife's death, "I got a counselor because I knew that I would need some help. He was great, particularly in helping me get rid of my guilt [about not being] perfect all the time." Television writer Carla Lane and another friend of Paul's, rock star Chrissie Hynde, visited him. Lane said, "Paul was just haggard. He sat there like an old man. He was shattered." Another friend, animator Geoff Dunbar, reported, "[Paul] was racked with grief . . . He sobbed like a baby." Seven hundred mourners attended Linda's memorial service at St. Martin-in-the-Fields church in Trafalgar Square, London.

Linda's was one of the precious few funerals that Paul, who, as we know, has never dealt well with death, has ever attended.

As in the aftermath of the Beatles breakup—his previous separation of great consequence, though not as consequential as this one—Paul retreated for a time, then reemerged. Musically, his first album back, which can now be seen as a precursor to regular glances in the rearview mirror, was a collection of gutbucket rock 'n' roll covers of songs he had sung as a Silver

In the aftermath of John's murder, Paul and Ringo are getting by with a little help from their friends, which of course includes each other. These are two photographs of musical—and personal—reunions. At top are Paul and George Martin, at just about the time of the release of their collaboration on *Tug of War* in 1982. At bottom are Paul and Ringo in 1984, when Paul's less successful *Give My Regards to Broad Street,* which has Ringo drumming on several tracks, is dropped. The recordings themselves hardly matter. The Beatles are okay again, and Paul is more than okay with this. There are marvelous clips to be seen on YouTube of Ringo and Paul visiting George at his house and jamming on the old numbers—even "Raunchy," which got young George his job in the band when Paul arranged the audition on the bus in front of Quarry Men leader John. That sunny afternoon at George's grand estate, though: The host is often on ukulele, and in Paul's most recent concerts, he sings "Something," accompanying himself on ukulele. It is a beautiful thing to see and hear.

In January of 1990, Paul and Linda are together and content. By this time, they have become symbols of certain things, the last of which will prove a cruel irony in the next few years: marital harmony in the world of rock, strength of character in the face of criticism and the pursuit of a healthy lifestyle through a vegetarian diet.

After Linda's death from breast cancer, Paul retreats once more, then reappears in a most unusual way. On December 17, 1998, he takes to the Internet and prepares his signature mashed potatoes, while speculating that he might want to become a TV chef one day. He accepts questions from fans around the world. Sir Paul says that he has shed more tears in the past year than he ever had in his life. He shows how Linda had taught him just the proper way to cut onions (opposite). He emphasizes that this is a vegetarian recipe assembled by his late wife, and implies that he will continue along the vegetarian course (which he has). He adds parsley. He is asked if Linda could play the guitar and admits: not very well, but she knew the chords A, D and E. He plays a music video. He shows photos of Linda. He is asked by a fan from Mexico if he will tour again, and answers, "Yes, I think I might. I like touring. Normally what happens is that I wait until the urge grabs me." For now, though, he is grieving, because, as he said in his only earlier public comment following Linda's death: "I just always fancied her and I think that's what's so difficult about losing her."

Beetle, plus originals sent, with love, to Linda. It was terrific music. On December 14, 1999, Paul played Liverpool's Cavern Club for the first time since 1963. He started turning up again at London charity functions, at Stella's fashion shows, even onstage. Too early for some (fans always feel that they have a vital stake in their hero's life), there was a new companion at his side, and in the summer of 2001 the activist Heather Mills became his fiancée. They would marry the following year, but in the interim . . .

On November 29, 2001, George Harrison died at 58 after three years spent fighting lung cancer. Paul was with him near the end. "We just sat there stroking hands," he said to Larry King afterward. "And this is a guy and . . . you don't stroke hands with guys like that . . . We just spent a couple of hours, and it was really lovely."

Ringo was in attendance at Paul and Heather's wedding at a castle in Ireland on June 11, 2002, as were George Martin, Paul's brother, Mike (standing up for him a second time), and Paul's daughters Mary and Stella—though it had been reported that none of the children were happy with the turn of events. On the inside of the McCartney orbit, there were many who simply didn't like Heather. Until she was 31, they would point out, she walked on the shady side, posing for porn photos. At 25, she lost her lower left leg in an accident—sad, unquestionably—and this incident led to a kind of celebrityhood where she became a regular on TV and in tabloids, advocating for injury survivors like herself. But it seemed plain to those in Paul's circle that his new heartthrob was not in love with him. "Ha!" said Mark Featherstone-Witty, CEO of the Liverpool Institute for Performing Arts. "I've met self-centered people in my life, but she has to get the gold star. She wins the Oscar for self-centered." Said Heather to Barbara Walters in a too-candid interview: "I am married to the most famous person in the world, and that is very unfortunate for me. When you become famous at 19, it is sometimes hard to listen to other people's suggestions." For Heather, who was said to prefer AC/DC to the Beatles, those

suggestions included putting her and her causes more to the fore. It wasn't happening; it couldn't happen—no one could upstage Paul McCartney in the 21st century. Discord came relatively quickly; shouting followed.

A lovely interlude, in the years when Paul tried to escape from the Sturm und Drang whenever he could: In early January 2005, none other than Keith Richards, the Rolling Stones guitarist, was climbing on the rocks outside his beach house on the Caribbean island of Parrot Cay. He looked up and, as he writes in his memoir, *Life,* "along the shore came Paul McCartney. It was certainly the strangest place for us to meet after all the years, but certainly the best, because we had time to talk, maybe for the first time since those earliest days . . . He said he'd found out where I lived from my neighbor Bruce Willis. He said, 'I hope it's OK. Sorry I didn't ring.'"

McCartney was kicking back before headlining the 2005 Super Bowl halftime show. "Paul started to turn up every day, when his kid was sleeping," writes Keith. (The kid would have been Paul and Heather's daughter, Beatrice, born in October 2003.) "I'd never known Paul that well. John and I knew each other quite well, and George and Ringo, but Paul and I had never spent much time together. We were really pleased to see each other. We fell straight in, talking about the past, talking about songwriting. We talked about such strangely simple things as the difference between the Beatles and the Stones . . . I dared him to play 'Please Please Me' at the Super Bowl, but he said they needed weeks of warning. I remembered his hilarious takeoff of Roy Orbison singing it, so we started singing it . . . We had a good time together."

But Paul and Heather weren't having any kind of good time together, and in the 2008 divorce proceedings Heather demanded £125 million. The accounting firm Ernst & Young assessed Paul's net worth at approximately £387 million, and she was awarded a lump sum payment of £16.5 million (the equivalent of $33 million at the time). Heather complained to the press that she had been short-changed. Paul had not too long before passed his 64th birthday, as in: "Will

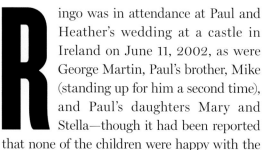

SEPTEMBER 24, 2003
CONCERT FOR GEORGE

Going forward is often about going back: Paul sits in a classroom at his old school, the Liverpool Institute (opposite); he stands in front of the Cavern Club stage, where he is to put on a show in 1999, his first performance at the club since 1963; he and his wife, Heather, join Ringo and his wife, Barbara Bach, at the 2003 premiere of a film saluting their late bandmate George—a movie in which Paul and Ringo, of course, figure prominently.

you still need me / Will you still feed me / When I'm 64?"

Nancy Shevell surely will, when he's 74—just a few years on. She, a businesswoman of accomplishment, is a serious and stalwart person, and she and Paul seem happy indeed. They spent time together as Paul's divorce was ongoing—she was then a 47-year-old soon-to-be divorcée, from an esteemed New York family (not too unlike Linda Eastman, once upon a time)—and began dating not long thereafter. In 2008 they took a cross-country road trip in a 1989 Ford Bronco along the route of old Route 66—Paul had always wanted to do that—and fell in love. "Route 66 was a wonderful experience," said Paul later, while also admitting that his plan, which included little more than a guitar, a tent and a map, was pretty much half-baked. "It could have been a disaster, but it turned out well and we had a great time. It certainly brings back lots of lovely memories." In 2011, Paul and Nancy became engaged and later in the year married. All good.

In the meantime, of course, music. There will never not be music. There are warhorses from the 1960s who are still writing and singing songs worth listening to. Bob Dylan, Paul Simon and Van Morrison are three, and Paul McCartney is a fourth. They are all still performing, too. The trim, vegetarian McCartney assays an annual schedule of concerts and benefits that would waste a person half his age: more than 30 songs each night (two thirds of them from the Beatles canon). His last several albums, including his most recent collaboration with producer Youth, a.k.a. Martin Glover, in their *Fireman* collaboration, have been terrific. The latest solo effort, conceived with Nancy in mind ("She was a great motivation and inspiration"), elicited this response from Miles Raymer, a contributor to *Pitchfork*, a music website targeted at the young: "It's gratifying and inspiring to see the pop musician who arguably most deserves to rest on his laurels steadfastly refuse to do so."

The name of that album?

New.

At right is a portrait of Paul in 2003. Everything he would do in the new millennium would delight his multitude of fans and irk his minority of detractors quite the same as everything he had done earlier already had. He would make whatever music he wanted to make, and much of it would be marvelous. A good case can be made that no pop singer-songwriter has had a better aesthetic run in this period than McCartney with *Chaos and Creation in the Backyard* (2005), *Memory Almost Full* (2007) and *New* (2013)—with the charming album of standards, *Kisses on the Bottom* (2012), plus his collaboration with Youth, interspersed. He would do what he wanted to do, whether his family wanted him to or not. (Ah, Heather.) He would find mature love. (Ah, Nancy.) Always, he would play on. One day he is placing his still supple voice onto a lyric written a half century ago, while the master jazz guitarist John Pizzarelli lays a filigree beneath, and the next he is screaming helter skelter while Dave Grohl slams away at his side. It's all music to Paul. Right now, everything's music to Paul.

It was 1964 when Paul McCartney and his three best friends first took the stage at the Ed Sullivan Theater in midtown Manhattan and affected cultural (and perhaps world) history. It is 45 years later when Paul returns to the scene of the crime and plays to a crowd on Broadway from atop the Sullivan Theater's marquee during an appearance on David Letterman's show. He sings "Get Back," "Helter Skelter," a couple other Beatles tunes, one from Wings. He is enjoying himself. The crowd is roaring. Then it seems his time is up. Paul leans in and says to a policeman, "Can we stay a little longer? Please?"

Harry Benson's

PAUL

One Photographer Remembers the Beatles, and Beyond

t was, to be specific, January 14, 1964, and the Scotsman Harry Benson was one of the sharp-elbowed young shooters employed by the tabloids—he was with the London *Daily Express*—which were headquartered, for the most part, up and down London's Fleet Street. Benson had been doing well and had just drawn a plum assignment: the ongoing wars in Africa. "I'd had all my shots," he remembers as he relaxes in his New York City apartment on a sunny autumn morning in 2013. "I was packed and ready to go. I got a call very late at night. It was the paper. 'We want you to do the Beatles. They're in Paris.' I told them I couldn't do it—I was going to Africa. I said to myself, 'I'm a serious, *serious* journalist. I'm going to Africa!' I hung up. Five minutes later, the phone rang again. It was the photo editor. 'The editor says you're going to Paris.' So I went to Paris. You do what you're told.

"I got there, and my first encounter with the Beatles was at the concert in Versailles. I was approaching from my car and I remember I heard that sound, 'Close your eyes and I'll kiss you . . .' And the screaming! I heard the screams and I thought, *Jesus, I'm on the right story.*"

He certainly was, and he stayed on it, longer than he might have imagined. He took the first of his many well-known Beatles photos in Paris when the band learned that "I Want to Hold Your Hand" had reached No. 1 in America, and Harry urged a reprise of the previous evening's pillow fight. Then he was headed for the airport with the boys, and his covering of the British Invasion from the inside. Afterward, though, he went off to other assignments. "We were friends, but I only go around a celebrity if there's a reason," he says. "The Beatles were important to my career, but the Beatles weren't 'my career.' Bobby Kennedy, the I.R.A., the Gulf War—these things were to be photographed." Benson photographed them, and many of his images made their way to—or were assigned by—LIFE.

The years went by, and circumstance brought him back in touch with the Beatles from time to time. He was in New York when John was killed. He was in England when a magazine needed a piece on Paul and Wings. Eventually, there was a portfolio as comprehensive and intimate as any. On these pages: selected images, and Harry's pithy commentary.

"Paul always knew where he was when the camera was going," says Harry. "Even all that time ago at the George V hotel in Paris [where the pictures on these pages and the previous one were taken] he knew how to be in the action. He made sure to be lively. He made the picture."

When Harry Benson was there, it's clear from his photographs that he wasn't a fly on the wall; he was right in the midst of whatever was happening and often helping to make it happen. Paul might be shaving on the plane, and Harry would draw him out. Paul might be having a private moment with Jane Asher, and then it wouldn't be quite so private (but would still be one of the most intimate photos of the couple ever made). The band would be deplaning in New York, and Harry, trailing them to the door of the airplane, would realize: This is the moment. He tells Ringo to get the others to turn around and, voilà—not only is a historic moment recorded but one of the most famous Beatles photographs ever is taken.

Of the photo above, taken in 1975, Harry recalls, "Linda and Paul were stoned, and they handed me the joint. Honest to God, I didn't inhale but pretended to. 'I'm glad you did that, Harry,' said Linda—meaning I was part of their world now." Whatever the basis for their trust, the McCartneys allowed Harry to make what are now very rare pictures of their family life. Below are pictures taken at home, including, at bottom, with daughter Mary in 1975; at right, same year: with Mary (left) and Stella.

Harry Benson, has been represented in LIFE since the 1960s, which is to say we know him, and he would not take any kind of umbrage at our assessment that he embodies a curious Scottish blend of openhearted sentimentality and crusty anti-sentimentality. "The picture on the white horse shows the kind of love between them," he says of this photograph, which was made in 1992 at the McCartney farm in East Sussex, England. "She was all right, Linda. She was okay." He pauses and adds, "I never shot the other one." That would have been Heather, but, as Harry says, she's not part of this portfolio. Harry's collection ends, for now, with Paul and Linda. Paul is still out there, rocking, playing, living a public life. Harry is still out there shooting. There is, for these two who were on that Pan Am flight 50 years ago as it touched down in Queens, still lots of time.

8/19/21 DC

8/19/21 DC